THE HIGHLY SENSITIVE YOUNG ADULT

A PRACTICAL GUIDE TO REDUCING OVERWHELM, DEALING WITH TOXIC PEOPLE, AND THRIVING IN YOUR WORK AND RELATIONSHIPS

JORDAN T. BECKETT

BOOKEDGE
PUBLISHING

Copyright © 2023 by Jordan T. Beckett - **All rights reserved.**

The content contained within this book may not be reproduced, duplicated or transmitted without direct written permission from the author or the publisher.

Under no circumstances will any blame or legal responsibility be held against the publisher, or author, for any damages, reparation, or monetary loss due to the information contained within this book. Either directly or indirectly. You are responsible for your own choices, actions, and results.

Legal Notice:

This book is copyright protected. This book is only for personal use. You cannot amend, distribute, sell, use, quote or paraphrase any part, or the content within this book, without the consent of the author or publisher.

Disclaimer Notice:

Please note the information contained within this document is for educational and entertainment purposes only. All effort has been executed to present accurate, up to date, and reliable, complete information. No warranties of any kind are declared or implied. Readers acknowledge that the author is not engaging in the rendering of legal, financial, medical or professional advice. The content within this book has been derived from various sources. Please consult a licensed professional before attempting any techniques outlined in this book.

By reading this document, the reader agrees that under no circumstances is the author responsible for any losses, direct or indirect, which are incurred as a result of the use of the information contained within this document, including, but not limited to, — errors, omissions, or inaccuracies.

CONTENTS

Introduction ix

1. THE TRUTH ABOUT BEING A HIGHLY SENSITIVE YOUNG ADULT 1
   Sensory Sensitivity vs. Sensory Processing Disorder 6
   Sensory Sensitivity vs. Neurodiversity 8
   Introverts or Extroverts? 9
   Where do we go from here? 9
   Journal Prompts 13

2. I'M JUST A KID, AND LIFE IS (SOMETIMES) A NIGHTMARE 15
   Sensory Sensitivity and Trauma 19
   The Autonomic Nervous System 21
   Complex Post-Traumatic-Stress-Disorder 23
   Where do we go from here? 28
   Journal Prompts 31

3. FOSTERING FULFILLING FRIENDSHIPS 33
   Emotional Intelligence 35
   Forming Healthy Friendships 38
   Where do we go from here? 45
   Journal Prompts 47

4. ENRICHING ROMANTIC RELATIONSHIPS 49
   Strengths of Highly Sensitive People in Relationships 51
   Getting to Know Yourself and Your Needs 53
   Communicating Your Needs 57

Tips for Loving a Highly Sensitive Person 61
Where do we go from here? 63
Journal Prompts 65

5. CLAIMING CONTROL OF YOUR COLLEGE LIFE & LIVING SITUATION 67
Maximizing Housing Opportunities & Creating a Calming Space 69
Manage Your Sleeping and Social Meter 73
Where do we go from here? 75
Journal Prompts 77

6. PROSPER IN YOUR PROFESSIONAL LIFE 79
Problems that Highly Sensitive People Face at Work 81
Being Successful on Your Own Terms 83
Navigating Performance Reviews 87
Potential Careers for Highly Sensitive Young Adults 88
Where do we go from here? 89
Journal Prompts 91

7. SQUASH SOCIAL MEDIA OVERWHELM 93
How Social Media Harms the Highly Sensitive 95
Experiencing News Overload 97
Using Social Media in a Healthy Manner 101
Practicing Mindfulness 102
Where do we go from here? 106
Journal Prompts 108

8. EXPERIENCING THE MIND-BODY CONNECTION 110
Harmful Thought Patterns and Cognitive Distortions 112
The Mind-Body Connection 116
Where do we go from here? 122
Journal Prompts 124

9. EMBRACING SELF-CARE 126
   Protecting Your Energy 128
   Sleep Hygiene 130
   Exercise as Time to Reflect and Recharge 133
   Taking Care of Your Mental Health 135
   Where do we go from here? 138
   Journal Prompts 140

   Conclusion 141
   Acknowledgments 147
   Journal Prompts 149
   About the Author 167
   Bibliography 169

For Scarlett

INTRODUCTION

In the early 2000s, there came a time, as there does for every good, Midwestern family, when it became imperative for my family to take a pilgrimage to Cedar Point. For those not yet initiated, Cedar Point is an amusement park in Sandusky, Ohio, which boasts seventy-one rides, most notably the *Millennium Force* and *Steel Vengeance*. Succumbing to and subsequently blacking out from the high velocity of such rides is a right of passage for many Midwestern adolescents. As we parked our dark blue mini-van in some forgotten corner of the 10-acre parking lot, I eagerly anticipated my turn.

Heat waves simmered as we trekked across the parking lot. I felt the blazing sun beating down on my shoulders and not in a fun, I'm-gonna-soak-up-the-sun type way. By the time we had made it to the Cedar Point sign at the front of the park, I was so sweaty I looked as if I had recently taken a nose dive into Lake Erie. My mom, insisting we get a group photo with Snoopy in front of the sign, was wildly gesticulating to passersby, hoping one would use her Sony point-and-shoot digital camera to take a group photo.

It was at this moment that my eagerness to pass under the arch and into the park began to falter. As a middle-aged woman with a fanny pack and a sun visor squatted to get us all in the frame, a rollercoaster whizzed passed our heads, carrying at least twenty screaming people. I gulped.

As the day progressed, I became increasingly overwhelmed and overstimulated. Why was the music so aggressively ear-splitting? Why was everyone talking so loud, and how could I get them to respect my personal space? Where could I find a shady spot to reprieve from the scorching sun?

My siblings gleefully ran back and forth between rides while I offered to "watch the bags." As they recounted their harrowing trips on each rollercoaster, I made a truly admirable effort not to check my Scooby-Doo watch. I wanted to go home. This place was too much. I couldn't think straight, couldn't catch my bearings. The environment of the amusement park was offensive to my senses. Don't get me wrong; I *wanted* to have a good experience. I had *wanted* to have a "normal response" to Cedar Point. What was wrong with me? How were my siblings enjoying this? Why wasn't I? Why am I like this?

Why am I like this?

This question haunted me for years. It became a mantra of sorts. A prayer I uttered to myself each time I sensed one of my responses to certain stimuli was atypical. As a child, I would become overwhelmed by a sensation or feeling and, not knowing how to process it, would bid my parents to help me navigate these big feelings. It was not often that they could, though, and little me would ask myself, "Why am I like this?" Why can't I be tougher? Why am I so needy?

By the time I was a teenager, my mantra had evolved from a prayer to a curse. I would spend countless nights staring at my ceiling, wondering what was wrong with me. There was an ache in my chest; something was missing. I know now that that "something" was part of my identity. There was a part of me I had yet to meet, a part of me that, once accepted, would change the way I perceived the world and would become a catalyst for creative endeavors.

You see, I am a Highly Sensitive Person (HSP), and my guess is, if you've picked up this book, you believe you may be one, too. We'll get more into the psychology and sociological implications of being an HSP later in the book, but for right now, I want you to know there is *nothing wrong with you*. You simply see the world in a different light than those whose sensory intake is considered typical. You have been given a unique gift because you were born without rose-colored glasses. You see the world at its face value and have the creativity and lived experience to make something beautiful of it.

I no longer am cursed by the "why am I like this?" monster. Instead, I see my sensitivity as a blessing. The real gift of being an HSP is once you accept this aspect of your personality, you harness the power to do extreme good. HSPs are the universe's great empathizers. We have a powerful capacity to understand sorrows because we have also been there. We dwell with others in their discomfort. We are willing to sit with pain and grief because we know that we are not fully human without these things. We desire to be fully, completely, and irrevocably *human*.

My ability to create, love myself and others, and cope with my feelings of anxiety and depression significantly abated after I learned more about my unique personality type. I've spent nearly a decade researching and studying the work of psychologists such as Carl Yung, philosophers such as Marcus Aurelius, and many more. Through these years of study and research, I have learned how to implement "HSP coping strategies," which help me live my life to the fullest without foregoing my proclivity to sensitivity.

This book's crosshairs are mainly targeted toward young adult HSPs between 18 and 29 years old, but the information here benefits anyone! I also hope you enjoy the stories throughout the book; however, certain names and specific details have been altered to preserve anonymity and respect the individual's privacy.

Throughout this book, I will guide you as you learn more about yourself and hand you a few new tools to help you navigate the world as an HSP.

Moving forward, this book will be split into two sections:

1. What You Need to Know: Learning what it means to be an HSP
2. What You Can Do About It: Practical steps toward decreasing sensory overload and increasing positive experiences

I hope this book will help alleviate your anxieties and calm your fears about the future. I hope to teach you how to decrease negative self-talk and rumination while increasing your capacity for positive connections.

I'm here to introduce you to a part of yourself you likely haven't met yet, a part of yourself that's easily wounded but capable of great and restorative things, a part of yourself that is often misunderstood by society and even sometimes ridiculed for being "too sensitive." I'm here to say: fear not, my friend, for society needs you.

So, what do you say? Ready to take the plunge?

THE TRUTH ABOUT BEING A HIGHLY SENSITIVE YOUNG ADULT

"I was ashamed of myself when I realized life is a costume party, and I attended with my own face."

— FRANZ KAFKA

It is a truth universally acknowledged that if your family owns a business, you'll likely end up working at said family business during the summers. Growing up, my family owned a lumber yard, and sometimes, when I close my eyes, I still feel the hot, Michigan humidity that filled my lungs as I loaded two-by-fours into some DIYers truck bed. If I concentrate hard enough when I rub my thumb across my palm, I can still feel the callouses once etched there, tender craters that remind me of time spent laboring with my family and the people employed at our lumber yard.

Typically, I got on well with everyone who worked in the yard. We'd spend our mornings checking and filling orders, often loudly blaring a local classic rock radio station. In the afternoon, we'd unwrap our wonder-bread sandwiches and spend time roasting each other in good fun. However, one summer, all was not peachy. We hired an employee for the summer named David. David was in his early twenties, and I knew something was off from the moment I met him. He swaggered everywhere with the confidence of someone much older than twenty-one. He spoke with a drawn-out California lilt, which I thought was odd, considering he'd grown up in Southeast Michigan. Still, he seemed to get along with everyone and dutifully completed his work.

I told my mom, who did the billing for the yard that something about David rubbed me the wrong way. She brushed it off, saying she got on well with him and that I was being "judgmental." Don't get me wrong, I didn't have it out for David, but my intuition told me to be wary of him. It was something in the way David carried himself, or maybe it was the *way* he said things, always taking the lunchtime teasing a little too far.

By the end of the summer, we had noticed team morale had significantly declined. People had started taking lunch alone in their cars and griping at each other while filling orders. I saw more eye-rolling and pointed glances during team meetings. Something was up, and my family couldn't determine what was bothering everyone. David's last day at the company came and went, and he moved away to start a graduate program.

The culture at the yard was still off, though, so my mom and one of the office managers decided to do a little digging. One by one, they'd pull an employee into the break room to get to the bottom of the bad vibes. Turns out, David had been pitting all of the employees against each other and against my family through one-on-one conversations and after-work texts. No one felt safe or at home anymore! They assumed everyone was gossiping about them with David.

I was shocked and angered by his actions. Furthermore, I was stunned at my uncanny ability to notice something was off with David moments after meeting him. How had I been able to pick up on the subtle cues and messages he had been sending? Was it his body language? The tone of voice? It wasn't until years later that I realized my ability to almost immediately pick up on these things was due to my highly sensitive personality.

Dr. Elaine Aron, the foremother of the study of highly sensitive personalities, states that Highly Sensitive People (HSPs) exhibit a unique ability to sense the world around them. This trait is often called "sensory processing sensitivity" or "environmental sensitivity," meaning every interaction an HSP has is magnified in terms of sound, smell, taste, and feel. People with the HSP personality trait are significantly affected by external stimuli compared to non-HSP people. According to Dr. Aron, this trait affects nearly 15-20% of the population, which means one in five people have "enhanced" sensory intake.

Highly sensitive personalities have long been considered an adaptation. As our ancestors foraged and hunted, processing one's surroundings more effectively and quickly became necessary. This trait has been passed down from generation to generation and is your brain's way of trying to help you stay alive. However, in today's society, it may seem more of a hindrance than an advantage. Often, when HSPs don't know how to manage this personality trait, they develop symptoms of emotional distress or may experience difficulties in their closest relationships. An inability to cope with sensory sensitivity may also lead to social anxiety and isolation.

It is important to note that there *are* benefits to having the highly sensitive personality trait in modern-day society. For instance, HSPs often have a rich inner life, meaning they can produce incredible works of art. Additionally, HSPs are emotionally intelligent and have a significant capacity for empathy. For example, I often find myself in a conversation, and by reading that person's body language and listening to their tone of voice, I can tell if they are uncomfortable, making it easier for me to reassure or comfort them.

People with sensory sensitivities can often determine they have the HSP trait through lived experiences. Maybe concerts or loud bars are too much for you to handle? Perhaps the cleaning products used at your office make you sick to your stomach or trigger headaches? Still, more concrete ways exist to determine if you are an HSP. If you're a personality test person, I encourage you to check out Dr. Aron's Highly Sensitive Self-test (found on her website).

HSPs also exhibit qualities such as:

- A low threshold for sensory intake
- High susceptibility to overstimulation or overwhelm
- Appearing "introverted" or "emotional"
- High levels of empathy
- Low pain tolerance

- Needing to "come down" after social interaction

At this point, you may be asking yourself: "What made me this way?" While each of us has unique experiences and genetic makeup, there is emerging research into the origin of sensory sensitivity overall. Psychologist, Elizabeth Scott, notes that sensory sensitivity may be linked to a lack of emotional connection with caregivers during childhood. She goes on to state that adverse childhood experiences may be a contributing factor to sensory sensitivity, as well. While sparse, data is emerging suggesting sensory sensitivity is hereditary, as well.

SENSORY SENSITIVITY VS. SENSORY PROCESSING DISORDER

When I first learned about sensory sensitivity, I wondered if I met the criteria for any specific diagnosis. I was curious if I had a disorder or if I was gifted "Spidey senses" (without the excruciating spider bite). Perhaps the most pressing question I had was if Sensory Sensitivity was synonymous with Sensory Processing Disorder. While there are similarities between the two conditions, there are also striking differences.

Sensory Processing Disorder (SPD) is when your brain over- or under-reacts to external stimuli. Remember, sensory stimuli consists of all you can taste, see, smell, feel, or hear. Neither Sensory Sensitivity nor Sensory Processing Disorder is included in the DSM-5 (a reference book on mental health and brain-related conditions and disorders). However, clinicians may diagnose children with SPD with Global developmental delay, a condition in which a child struggles to interpret and organize external stimuli effectively, thus limiting their responses or delaying their response time. It is important to note Global developmental delay is a diagnosis given to children; psychiatrists may change this diagnosis as a child matures, and new diagnostic techniques may be introduced.

HSP's sensory sensitivity enables them to respond appropriately in social situations, even when overwhelmed. As opposed to people with SPD, HSPs rarely experience under-stimulation from external stimuli. This divergence is the easiest way to differentiate between the two conditions. Those with SPD may be unable to respond appropriately when overwhelmed, meaning they may come across as bizarre or antisocial. If either of these conditions resonate with you, I highly recommend speaking with a licensed therapist or primary care physician.

SENSORY SENSITIVITY VS. NEURODIVERSITY

People with Autism Spectrum Disorder (ASD) and Attention-deficit-hyperactivity Disorder (ADHD) may experience similar "symptoms" to HSPs, as well. However, it is important to note that sensory sensitivity does not indicate ASD or ADHD. It may be, in some instances, that a neurodivergent person is highly sensitive, but, as with SPD, having a highly sensitive personality does not affect a person's quality of life as being neurodivergent might.

The primary difference between neurodiversity and sensory sensitivity is the type of sensitivity they experience. For instance, people with ASD may experience either hyper- or hypo-sensitivity, meaning they can have increased or decreased physiological responses to external stimuli. HSPs, do not experience hypo-sensitivity and, therefore, as I mentioned earlier, will not experience under-stimulation due to their sensory sensitivity. HSPs can quickly interpret another person's motives or meaning behind their words, while people with ASD may struggle to do so. As before, if any of these conditions resonates with you, I encourage you to speak with a licensed therapist or your doctor.

INTROVERTS OR EXTROVERTS?

At face value, it may appear that HSPs *must* be introverts. However, only 70% of sensitive people are introverts. Often, HSPs must be alone to "come down," or their desire for quiet spaces may be interpreted as introversion. That being said, sensory sensitivity does affect extroverts, as well. Their sensitivity does not affect their socialization capacity, so a person can actually be extroverted and highly sensitive. As touched on earlier, HSPs tend to be communication whizzes. They read body language well and may often "referee" social gatherings in an effort to ensure everyone is included. An extroverted HSP may be the life of the party and may be recharged by socialization. However, as an extroverted HSP, they still may need to schedule a time to recharge after social engagements.

WHERE DO WE GO FROM HERE?

At the beginning of this chapter, I quoted Franz Kafka. I chose this quote because I felt it exemplified the HSP experience. As a highly sensitive person, I often feel that everyone else is experiencing the world with a protective barrier. They are protected from bright lights, loud noises, and the fatigue of constantly interpreting another's motives, whereas I have shown up to the party in my birthday suit, without any protective barriers.

Often, these feelings of vulnerability have affected my mental health and relationships. To show up hyperaroused is to show up at max capacity. How can I connect with the person sitting across from me at the coffee shop if I'm focused on the volume of the music, the smell of the person's deodorant behind me, and the feeling of having too many bodies crammed into one space?

The good news is life as an HSP gets much easier once you have a basic understanding of how your brain works and how to manage your sensitivity. As you begin brainstorming on how to engage with your life as an HSP, I encourage you to think of your five senses. Consider getting blue light-blocking glasses or ensuring you always have sunglasses before leaving home. You might consider rummaging through your closet; what do your favorite clothes look and feel like? What items do you own that you *hate* wearing? Lastly, I encourage you to seek psychotherapy if you deem it appropriate. Licensed therapists have so many tools to help you on this journey! If you don't know how to access a therapist, I suggest discussing this desire with a physician.

SOMETHING instrumental in aiding my social life has been creating a "come down" routine. This practice has helped decrease my social anxiety before an event and helps prevent me from ruminating or being on edge for hours after it's over. It could be as simple as creating a checklist in the notes app on your phone.

Currently, my preferred come-down routine is as follows:

1. Put on some calming music
2. Take a shower
3. Whisper sweet-nothings to my houseplants
4. Make some tea
5. Read or journal

The wonderful thing is this routine can be unique to you! This could be something you do every day after work or after dinner at a loud restaurant with friends. Try it for a week or two to see how it helps you cope with overwhelming feelings.

Throughout the rest of this book, we will walk through the "highlights" of your life. We'll take a peek at the childhood experiences of HSPs. You'll learn how to navigate romantic relationships, college, and your professional life as a sensitive young adult. Lastly, we'll look at some tried-and-true coping strategies to help you live as fully and deeply as possible. At the end of each chapter, there will be journal prompts to work through (it may be helpful for you to invest in a journal at this point!). If that's not for you, no worries! I only ask that you brainstorm a few ways to process what we're learning together as we progress throughout this book.

> *To be highly sensitive is to be deeply aware of the fact that you are alive.*

Take some time to think about a typical day in your own life. Can you think of any times when your HSP trait revealed itself throughout the day? What sounds do you hear when you first wake up? Does the smell of petrichor as you step outside in the morning fill you with joy? As stated earlier, the ability to notice environmental minutiae may be exhausting. However, I must remind you that you can catch the world in all its glory. Author Kurt Vonnegut wrote, "And I urge you to please notice when you are happy, and exclaim, or murmur, or think at some point, 'If this isn't nice, I don't know what is.'" Happy noticing.

∼

JOURNAL PROMPTS

- *Reflect on a time when you had a strong intuition about someone or a situation, similar to the author's experience with David. What subtle cues or messages did you pick up on? How did your highly sensitive personality contribute to your ability to sense something was off?*

- *Explore your relationship with sensory sensitivity. Think about the different senses (sound, smell, taste, touch, sight) and how they affect you daily. Describe a specific situation where you felt overwhelmed or overstimulated by external stimuli. How did you cope with it? Are there any strategies or techniques you can implement to manage sensory sensitivity in the future?*

- *Consider the benefits and challenges of being a highly sensitive person in today's society. What are some advantages of having enhanced sensory intake? On the other hand, what difficulties have you faced due to sensory sensitivity? How have these experiences affected your closest relationships and well-being?*

- *How did you come to realize that you have a highly sensitive personality? Reflect on the emotions and thoughts that surfaced when you discovered this aspect of your identity. How has this knowledge impacted your perception of yourself and your place in the world?*

I'M JUST A KID, AND LIFE IS (SOMETIMES) A NIGHTMARE

"Most of our childhood is stored not in photos, but in certain biscuits, lights of day, smells, textures of carpet.

— ALAIN DE BOTTON

I distinctly remember the smell of my grandmother's carpet: mothballs, her dog, Gidget, and a hint of minestrone soup. I remember these vivid smells because I spent many an hour with my rug-burned face pressed into the carpet as I gasped, "Uncle! Uncle!" My older brother, a rough-and-tumble kid, *loved* to wrestle. I, on the other hand, would have much rather preferred being a spectator to the ThunderDome-esque smackdowns that ensued at Grandma's.

It was during these childhood smackdowns that I realized I might be *different*. Take my brother, for example, who is self-confident and aggressive. As I watched him navigate life, I realized I was the opposite: withdrawn, agreeable, and *sensitive*. Soon, other children also began to notice these traits, and I was frequently bullied for my sensitive personality. I often felt ostracized, teased, and left out because I didn't participate like "normal" children did in my childhood.

Now that I'm an adult, I see I was not an abnormal child but simply highly sensitive. Still, my experience is not uncommon. All too often, highly sensitive children are labeled as melodramatic, apprehensive, or peculiar. These societal labels often lead to social ostracization, which can, in turn, lead to delayed psychosocial development.

According to psychotherapist Jenna Fleming, several traits are unique to HSP children, which include:

- Feeling overwhelmed by sensory stimuli
- Asking a lot of questions
- Being hyper-aware of changes in mood or atmosphere
- Being easily impacted by others' emotions
- Being intuitive & perceptive
- Having high empathy for others

- Having high sensitivity to pain
- Having strong clothing preferences
- Enjoying quiet activities compared to loud ones
- Having anxiety about new situations
- Being shy and introspective

The ability to process emotional exhaustion and sensory overwhelm is a learned behavior, which means children often exhibit "negative" behaviors while navigating big emotions. Furthermore, HSP children may be labeled as "bad seeds" due to their propensity to throw tantrums or because of their perceived social defiance. So, if you were a child who was often told you were a delinquent, please know that it may be because you had not yet been given the tools to process your sensitivities.

You are not a bad person.

While being bullied is not specific to highly sensitive children, they may be prone to experiencing it at higher rates, likely decreasing their self-esteem. This decrease in self-esteem may open the door for psychological issues and emotional burnout and may even impact a child's capacity for learning.

For instance, I was a decent student growing up. I

was never at the top of my class but was often placed somewhere in the middle. However, my teacher introduced math drills in the second grade to help us learn multiplication. We would stand in two lines, and she would roll a pair of giant, fluffy Las Vegas dice. The two children at the front of the line would have to race to see who could come up with the correct answer, with the loser moving to the back of the line.

I *hated* this game. Not because I wasn't good at multiplication; I was actually pretty fast. I just wasn't very fond of the game's competitive nature and that it had to be played under a time crunch in front of the entire class. What if I messed up and looked stupid in front of everyone? I disliked this game so much that I pretended I hadn't finished my other homework and couldn't participate. I thought I was pulling one over on Mrs. Bleek, but I'm sure she likely let me pretend because she was aware of my sensitive demeanor.

I know it may seem that HSP children have a decreased quality of life due to their tendency for emotional burnout and the probability of being left out socially. However, HSP children can have magical childhoods, provided their guardians show them acceptance, encouragement, social guidance, and emotional coping skills. Highly sensitive children often grow up to be creative, empathetic leaders, so please remember that despite what you may have experienced during childhood, you *do* belong, and we need you here!

SENSORY SENSITIVITY AND TRAUMA

In a perfect world, every child would have guardians who consistently encouraged them, accepted them, and modeled appropriate behavior for them. However, it is not a perfect world we live in, and the people around us are especially flawed. As Plato wrote, "Be kind, for everyone you meet is fighting a hard battle." We each cope with this hard battle in different ways: some of us learn healthy mechanisms, while others never gain the capacity to consistently and healthily cope. Furthermore, the fact is that perfect people never become parents because perfect people do not exist. No matter who raised you, there likely came a time when your parent or guardian misunderstood you, or made you feel "other", for how you reacted to certain things. Perhaps you were abused or neglected by those who were supposed to protect and care for you. If this happened, know I am deeply sorry; you didn't deserve that, and I wish you peace.

NEXT, I want to discuss sensory sensitivity and trauma because HSPs can be so profoundly affected by traumatic experiences, especially during childhood. As HSPs have more delicate sensory receptors, trauma and the subsequent emotions and physiological symptoms can seriously impact an HSP's quality of life.

So, first, what is trauma? According to the American Psychological Association, trauma "is an emotional response to a terrible event, like an accident, assault, or natural disaster." Experiencing trauma can lead to lasting emotional and even physiological symptoms (i.e., depression or chronic fatigue). Over time, these feelings of hyperarousal wreak havoc on the nervous system, often meaning a traumatized person is in "fight-or-flight" mode.

According to the National Library of Medicine, symptoms of trauma include:

- Exhaustion
- Confusion
- Sadness
- Anxiety
- Agitation
- Numbness
- Dissociation

- Confusion
- Physical arousal
- Blunted affect

It was Benjamin Franklin who said that "the only sure things in life are death and taxes." Well, I'd like to add a third: *trauma*. All of us, at one time or another, will experience trauma. It looks different for everyone, and we each will attempt to cope with our experiences in diverse ways. If you experienced traumatic events as a child, or if this is the first time you're allowing yourself to wonder if you have experienced trauma, I encourage you to speak to a licensed professional. They can help you unpack your experiences and emotions healthily and sustainably.

THE AUTONOMIC NERVOUS SYSTEM

My friend, Aubrey, went to therapy for the first time after she lived through a traumatic experience at work. Without going into specifics, a person unexpectedly and tragically died at her workplace, and Aubrey kept reliving that day over and over. Whenever she closed her eyes, she saw that person's face, witnessing the fear and panic in her coworkers' eyes as they processed what was happening. She became incredibly anxious, unable to sleep or eat properly, and struggled even to enter the room where the incident occurred. Desperate to relieve this cycle of horrific images, she booked a session with a local therapist.

After spending time getting to know her, the therapist immediately presented Aubrey with a graphic of the Autonomic Nervous System. According to the Cleveland Clinic, the Autonomic Nervous System (ANS) "is a subsystem of the peripheral nervous system, which encompasses all the nerve tissue in the body except the brain and spinal cord." The ANS consists of two parts: the sympathetic nervous system and the parasympathetic nervous system. The sympathetic nervous system is responsible for the "fight-or-flight" response mentioned earlier. When stimulated, it manifests as dilated pupils, dry mouth, constricted breathing, rapid heartbeat, and muscle tension.

Conversely, the parasympathetic nervous system is like a chill, relaxed surfer. When stimulated, your parasympathetic nervous system allows for slowed heart rate, steady breathing, and muscle relaxation. Both nervous systems exist to keep you alive. However, once traumatized, people often struggle to regulate their nervous system, meaning they spend much time hyperaroused.

During her post-traumatic event therapy sessions, the therapist informed Aubrey that she had to relearn how to activate her parasympathetic nervous system, which would help alleviate the feelings of terror and help her cope with what she had experienced. As a highly sensitive person, she realized it was even more imperative to do so because, as Dr. Judith Orloff states, "[Being an HSP] is like feeling with fifty fingers as opposed to ten. You have more receptors to perceive things."

Aubrey and her therapist then brainstormed ways to calm her sympathetic nervous system. For her, that looked like taking regular walks to enjoy nature, getting some sun, journaling, and ensuring she ate regularly. Through therapy and these practices, she was able to move through this traumatic event. It's still there; she still remembers exactly how she felt the day it happened, but it doesn't fill her with terror like it once did. She explained to me; it's akin to shopping for mass-produced souvenirs in beach towns: she can walk down the aisles of her memories, pick one up, and recognize that it does have some meaning, but it's not worth the price she's being asked to pay. She is now able to put it down and continue walking the aisles.

COMPLEX POST-TRAUMATIC-STRESS-DISORDER

When someone who has lived through a traumatic event experiences periods of significant hyperarousal, a clinician may diagnose them with Post-traumatic-stress-disorder (PTSD), a diagnosis with which most of us are familiar. Typically, PTSD is a diagnosis given to people who have experienced one specific traumatic event (i.e., assault or battery, car crashes, etc.). Symptoms of PTSD include avoiding people or situations that remind a person of the traumatic event they experienced, dizziness or nausea, hyperarousal, insomnia, suicidality, and loss of trust or close relationships.

In recent years, clinicians have been discussing and studying something called Complex Post-traumatic-stress-disorder (CPTSD), which, according to the team at Medical News Today, usually occurs "when a person experiences repeated trauma over an extended period of time." CPTSD is not currently recognized in the DSM-5 but is included in the ICD-11, the eleventh edition of the International Classification of Diseases, a tool used by physicians and other relevant healthcare workers.

CPTSD and PTSD have similar symptoms, but clinicians have provided additional symptoms for those diagnosed with CPTSD. Those diagnosed with

CPTSD may struggle to create and maintain close relationships, manage emotions, or may have strong feelings of guilt or worthlessness. Those with CPTSD may also experience significant physiological symptoms, such as headaches, chest pains, or stomach aches.

As it is accrued over extended periods, CPTSD is often triggered by childhood experiences, such as physical or emotional abuse, physical or emotional neglect, or sexual abuse. However, CPTSD can be triggered by any extended traumatic incident, such as prolonged domestic violence in an adult relationship.

I've decided to discuss trauma, specifically CPTSD, not because HSPs are more susceptible to traumatic events, but because the effects of such trauma can be incredibly magnified in an HSP's psyche. As an HSP's nervous system is more and more aroused, its ability to cope and engage in the outside world significantly decreases. For instance, as HSPs are more aware of sensory stimuli, certain smells may remind them of traumatic events and trigger an emotional or physical response, leading them to avoid similar situations in the future.

This can be especially relevant for HSPs with CPTSD caused by their childhood experiences. It feels almost as if they're delayed as adults. Someone who experienced prolonged emotional or physical neglect will have to work toward reparenting themselves as adults.

While an HSP's peers are getting married or having children, they're likely working on simply identifying their emotions at any
given time.

This can be incredibly overwhelming for HSPs, who may feel like others can't fathom the work they have to put into improving their quality of life.

Often, clinicians will use a tool called the Adverse Childhood Experience (ACE) survey to determine the intensity and type of trauma incurred during childhood before the age of eighteen. This survey's tallies, called ACE scores, cover such things as abuse, neglect, and household dysfunction. Below is a survey produced by Harvard's Center on the Developing Child.

The total number of "yes" answers at the end of the survey determines your ACE score:

1. Did a parent or other adult in the household often or very often… Swear at you, insult you, put you down, humiliate you, or act in a way that made you afraid you might be physically hurt?

2. Did a parent or other adult in the household often or very often... Push, grab, slap, or throw something at you? Or ever struck or injured you?
3. Did an adult or person at least five years older than you ever... Touch or fondle you, have you sexually touch their body? Or attempt or actually have oral, anal, or vaginal intercourse with you?
4. Did you often or very often feel that ... No one in your family loved you or thought you were important or special? Or did your family not look out for each other, feel close to each other, or support each other?
5. Did you often or very often feel that ... You didn't have enough to eat, had to wear dirty clothes, and had no one to protect you? Or were your parents too drunk or high to take care of you or take you to the doctor if you needed it?
6. Were your parents ever separated or divorced?
7. Was your mother or stepmother often or very often pushed, grabbed, slapped, or had something thrown at her? Or sometimes, often, or very often kicked, bitten, hit with a fist, or hit with something hard? Or ever

repeatedly hit over at least a few minutes or threatened with a gun or knife?
8. Did you live with anyone who was a problem drinker or alcoholic or who used street drugs?
9. Was a household member depressed or mentally ill, or did a household member attempt suicide?
10. Did a household member go to prison?

After reading through the ACE survey, it may be that new, upsetting emotions or memories revealed themselves. As an HSP, your symptoms are magnified every time you relive one of these memories. Like Aubrey's traumatic work experience, this cycle of rumination and reliving will likely repeat itself until it is interrupted. I encourage you to reach out to trusted loved ones and licensed clinicians with these emotions and memories.

WHERE DO WE GO FROM HERE?

In his short story *What We Talk About When We Talk About Love,* Raymond Carter writes,

> "I could hear my heart beating. I could hear everyone's heart. I could hear the human

noise we sat there making, not one of us moving, not even when the room went dark."

Similarly, I went to a conference on team building as a young professional, during which the keynote speaker had an arena full of people collectively holding their breath and releasing it after ten seconds. "There," he remarked, "we are one team. Our heartbeats are in syncopation."

This is not an abnormal occurrence, I think. We forget it, but our hearts all beat to similar tunes; we want love, belonging, and safety. We are all trying to navigate the time we've been given on Earth. Sometimes, unfortunately, traumatic experiences befall us as we make our journey. Sadly, these experiences sometimes happen to us as children, when we are most fragile and vulnerable.

Still, I genuinely believe beauty can still blossom, even after tragedy. In Japan, artists have practiced the art of Kintsugi for thousands of years. Kintsugi is the practice of repairing shattered and damaged pottery with a golden lacquer made of tree sap as opposed to using materials that would hide the cracks and breakage. The result is a unique piece of art that proudly showcases where it was once shattered. Each crack is filled with gold and is uniquely beautiful. It's similar to humans, I believe. We don't *have* to make our experiences beautiful, and we certainly don't have to list our adverse experiences as "personal development." It's true, though, that something can be made out of what was once shattered. If you so choose, you too can craft a beautiful piece of art from fragmented pieces.

∽

JOURNAL PROMPTS

- Reflect on a vivid childhood memory that is tied to a specific smell, texture, or sensory experience. Describe the memory and how it made you feel. How does this memory reflect your unique experiences as a child?

- Think about a time when you felt different or misunderstood compared to other children. How did this realization impact your self-perception and interactions with others? How did you navigate the challenges of being labeled as "different" or "sensitive"?

- Consider the unique traits of highly sensitive children provided by psychotherapist Jenna Fleming. Which of these traits resonate with you? How have these traits influenced your experiences? Reflect on how these traits can be seen as strengths rather than weaknesses.

- Reflect on a time when you faced a challenging situation that triggered your sensitivity. How did you react, and what emotions did you experience? How did you cope with the situation and process *your feelings? Describe any strategies or coping mechanisms that helped you navigate your sensitivity.*

FOSTERING FULFILLING FRIENDSHIPS

"I get by with a little help from my friends."

— THE BEATLES

In college, I started dating a beautiful and charismatic girl named Erica. After a month or so of things progressing well, it came time for her to meet my friends, so we decided that she would accompany me to one of my friend's birthday parties, where I could introduce her to the group. She was a little shy at first but soon warmed up to everyone. As she got more comfortable, she revealed more of her charismatic personality, and I was convinced they all adored her as much as I did. After meeting her, they confided in me that they thought she was a fun and supportive girl.

Fast forward a few months, I noticed my friends had stopped inviting Erica and me to outings and get-togethers. This upset me initially, but I just chalked it up to everyone being busy.

For unrelated reasons, Erica and I decided to go our separate ways. After we had broken up, I started getting invited to hang out with my friends again. At the next party, I pulled one of them aside and asked why they had avoided inviting Erica and me to things when we were together. "Oh," he said, "honestly, we just noticed that the vibe was different when you guys were together. I guess we didn't want to hurt your feelings because you said you really liked her." I think my jaw hit the floor. "You know you guys could've talked to me! You're my friends!"

Perhaps you, too, have had a similar experience. One in which your friends avoided communicating their true thoughts or desires with you out of fear of hurting your feelings. Maybe you've been betrayed by someone you considered a close friend, or you often feel you are giving more than receiving in your close friendships.

As I matured, I learned how to navigate these bumps with friends. I've also taken the time to learn how to identify people who will become authentic friends.

Together, let's take a look at what it means to be an HSP in friendships and how to navigate both positive and negative relationships.

EMOTIONAL INTELLIGENCE

There are several factors to consider when building friendships as a highly sensitive young adult. The first is Emotional Intelligence (EQ), which is your ability to recognize and understand emotions in yourself and others. Emotionally intelligent people use this awareness to manage their behavior and relationships, as well. Emotional intelligence is not unique to HSPs, but HSPs use their EQ to navigate life a little differently, and this difference can have incredibly positive and negative outcomes.

We've learned earlier that HSPs experience the world more intensely, so it makes sense that their increased reception of external stimuli would affect their social and parasocial relationships. For instance, a non-HSP can read facial expressions or take cues from another's body language. However, an HSP is likely listening to the cadence of another's footfalls, monitoring their breathing, or contemplating their word choice.

According to author and Emotional Intelligence Mentor, Shannan Callarman, emotional intelligence comprises four main factors: self-knowledge, self-management, relationship building, and social connection. Self-knowledge is the first ability to identify what you may feel during a social situation, an innate ability for HSPs. As HSPs "feel" first, they often begin to gauge the emotional "temperature" of any room they enter.

While an HSP can be affected by the emotional temperature of a room, they can easily manage their emotions, making them excellent at navigating emergency situations. HSPs often play peacemakers in social situations. Their increased ability to empathize helps them identify the feelings of both parties.

This increased ability to empathize lends itself well to relationship building, the third aspect of emotional intelligence. The ability to understand and make space for the feelings and needs of others is foundational to building healthy relationships. This ability is why, often, HSPs are readily accepted and is what may lead others to reveal personal information to HSPs so quickly. Have you ever experienced this in your day-to-day life?

> *When you start a new job, do coworkers easily latch on to you or reveal significant things about themselves or their past to you? Do you find that grocery clerks or bank tellers have more in-depth interactions with you?*

I have a friend who jokes that they always have to factor in a time buffer when they go out to eat with me because our waiter will likely tell me their life story.

An HSPs habitual attention to detail lends itself to impeccable active listening skills, allowing for more open dialogue. This fits in well with the fourth pillar of emotional intelligence: social connection. HSP's close friends often feel supported and understood and may often turn to their HSP for advice or direction. Their increased capacity for empathy also means that an HSP has the uncanny ability to tune in to what a person needs, sometimes even before that person has identified their own need.

It should be noted that there can be downfalls to having such well-developed emotional intelligence. For instance, HSPs may often find themselves playing the part of the "counselor" or trusted advisor for friends, family, and coworkers.

While it is good to have authenticity and vulnerability in relationships, it should be noted that one person can't be everything to everyone, always.

HSPs are susceptible to significant burnout and emotional exhaustion due to their high EQ. They may even fall victim to trauma by association.

Hear this, my friend; it is okay to support your

loved ones as they find a licensed clinician to help them navigate significant life events or emotions.

We'll delve into setting healthy boundaries shortly. Still, for now, I want you to know that your emotions and feelings matter, too. It's good to be a listening ear for those around you, but pay special attention to the people who want to hear about *you*, too.

FORMING HEALTHY FRIENDSHIPS

An unfortunate side effect of being a highly sensitive young adult is that you'll probably spend much of your time prioritizing other peoples' comfort in place of your own. As mentioned before, an HSP's emotional intelligence may, in turn, cause them to become the primary emotional support for their friends and loved ones. Because of this, HSPs must learn to form and sustain life-giving friendships. Our journey to healthy friendships then diverges into two sections: *forming healthy friendships* and *dissolving unhealthy friendships.*

HSPs, at their core, prefer depth over distance, quality over quantity, often requiring only a few close friends. Certainly, if they're extroverted, their social circles may be large, but there will only ever be a handful of people who genuinely know HSPs. They want to feel accepted and at peace in their friendships. They want a deep emotional connection. This can sometimes be difficult for HSPs; after all, it takes time to form and grow deep and lasting bonds. Often, this desire may be extinguished due to previous emotional burnout from unhealthy friendships. What's the point of expending all that emotional energy if it won't be reciprocated, leading, once again, to emotional burnout?

If this sounds like you, don't worry; you can find lasting and fulfilling friendships. In Psychology Today, Deborah Ward, a Licensed Clinical Social Worker, suggests looking for people you can trust when building friendships or relationships is essential. Trust is defined as a "firm belief in the reliability, truth, ability, or strength of someone or something." So, essentially, to trust in a person is to trust that they are who they say they are and will do what they say they will do. I know I know... Easier said than done, right?

I think it's important to recognize that friendships and trust take time to build. It's easy to get swept up in day-to-day responsibilities and forget to schedule an intentional time to "build trusting friendships." How does one even begin to build trust?

To be authentic is to know yourself and to be true to that person.

Living authentically means establishing personal

values and doing your best to adhere to them daily. To be authentic in relationships and friendships is to maintain these personal values despite the ever-present orbit of your loved ones and their influence. These values dictate how you will or will not spend your time, money, or physical/emotional capacities. For instance, if you've decided you value peace of mind, you may choose to unfollow any social media presence that makes you feel anxious or self-conscious and subsequently negatively affect your coveted peace of mind. *When you show up authentically, you can be loved authentically.* When people know where you stand, they see the posture to take when they stand with you.

Next, work on increasing your willingness to be vulnerable. To be emotionally vulnerable is to show yourself wholeheartedly and *authentically* even though you're fearful you may be hurt or rejected. Trust and vulnerability are similar to the age-old chicken vs. egg thought experiment. Which came first? The chicken or the egg? Trust or vulnerability? In my opinion, they are two sides of the same coin. As you spend time with someone, you begin to trust them and have what I've deemed "pick axe" conversations. Pick axe conversations are those intermittent and intimate conversations with another person that slowly chip away at who they are and what they've experienced. These pick-axe conversations allow you to express more vulnerability, thus building trust.

The third tenant to building trust is communication, both in frequency and in-depth. As I've mentioned, adulthood responsibilities can often prohibit us from intentionally communicating with those around us. Practice intentionally reaching out to current friends or people you wish to get to know. It can be as simple as sending them a text to check in or inviting them to a task you already do daily (i.e., taking a walk, getting lunch, etc.). Remember that, like you, the people you interact with want to be seen and heard. To facilitate deeper connections, practice asking intentional or open-ended questions and authentically responding when someone asks you about yourself.

Lastly, you must set healthy boundaries with friends and loved ones. The word "boundaries" can seem daunting or menacing, but I promise it's not as scary as it sounds. Dr. Sharon Martin states, "Boundaries are limits and expectations that we set for ourselves and others. They help both parties understand how to behave – what is acceptable and what isn't. Without boundaries, there are no rules of engagement – you're not sure how you want to be treated, and people aren't sure how to treat you! Elizabeth Earnshaw, a Licensed Marriage and Family Therapist, reports that there are six types of healthy boundaries: physical boundaries, emotional boundaries, time boundaries, sexual boundaries, intellectual boundaries, and material boundaries.

Let's look at some examples of each type of boundary:

Physical Boundaries
Problem: You realize that you often get distracted at work and end up having to stay late to get work completed. You notice that you spend much time chit-chatting with your coworkers in your office during the work day.
Boundary: You let your coworkers know that you'd love to catch up with them when your office door is open, but you have a project or task you need to prioritize when the door is closed.

Emotional Boundaries
Problem: You have been dealing with your mental health challenges lately, focusing on self-care and seeking professional help. You've been attending therapy sessions regularly to work through your personal issues and regain a sense of stability. However, one of your closest friends has relied heavily on you for emotional support during their recent breakup.
Boundary: You genuinely care about your friend and understand the importance of being there for them. However, you recognize that your mental health should

be a priority now. You kindly explain to your friend that you are working through your challenges and need to focus on your well-being. You suggest alternative sources of support for them, such as recommending a therapist or counselor or suggesting that they reach out to other friends or family members who may be available to provide support. You express your willingness to reconnect and offer support once you are better positioned to do so.

Time Boundaries
<u>Problem</u>: You have a doctor's appointment scheduled after work, but the person scheduled for the next shift is a no-show. Your boss tells you you'll have to wait until they arrive before you can leave. Normally, you're okay with working a little extra, but you really need to go to your doctor's appointment.
<u>Boundary</u>: You let your boss know that you're open to pre-scheduled overtime and are happy to cover shifts when coworkers communicate the need. However, you have a prior commitment and are unable to do so today.

Sexual Boundaries
<u>Problem</u>: Your partner attempts to initiate sex, but you're not feeling up for it.
<u>Boundary</u>: You let them know you're not in the mood

right now and ask if you can do something else together.

Intellectual Boundaries
Problem: It's Thanksgiving Day, and your extended family is gathered around the table. You're sitting next to your Uncle Ron, who's attempting to initiate a conversation about politics. You know your family has differing opinions, which could lead to a considerable disagreement and/or food fight.
Boundary: You struggled to get the mashed potatoes out of your hair after last year's melee, so you say, "Uncle Ron, I am uncomfortable talking about this during a family get-together. Can we discuss it at a later date, preferably when there's no food within grabbing distance?"

Material Boundaries
Problem: Your roommate uses your pots and pans without asking, and you notice they don't clean and put them away promptly.
Boundary: You request that they have your dishes cleaned and returned within the day, or you politely ask them to forgo using your pots and pans entirely.

Think about your life with these six types of boundaries in mind. In which areas are you most comfortable setting boundaries? Is there an area in which your boundaries aren't firm or consistently get crossed? Now, think of the people in your life. Can you identify anyone who consistently respects your boundaries? Who doesn't?

Now, there may come a day when you decide someone is not respecting your established boundaries. What options do you have? Suppose you feel that you have communicated your boundaries several times, and they're consistently being disrespected. In that case, it may be time to consider ending that friendship or relationship. This is much easier said than done, so please take your time and seek guidance if needed.

WHERE DO WE GO FROM HERE?

In 2011, a group of psychology students at Bethany Lutheran College in Mankato, Minnesota, decided to experiment on social conformity. The students surveyed by standing "backward" in an elevator at a local mall. They decided to see what people would do when they entered the elevator, and everyone was facing away from the doors. These students found several responses from study participants; some people conformed by facing the same way as everyone else, while others half-turned to appease their psychological need to conform without fully conforming.

According to Psychology Today, conformity is "the tendency for an individual to align their attitudes, beliefs, and behaviors with those around them. In many ways, this elevator experiment is indicative of the human experience. We take on the posture of those closest to us. Especially for HSPs, we can easily be swayed when our heartstrings are pulled or when we are in an unfamiliar environment. It becomes imperative, then, that we truly know ourselves and learn to identify our values. We must constantly show up authentically, despite the fear of rejection. We must communicate who we are, so we can be loved for all our quirks and strengths.

In their song "With a Little Help From My Friends", The Beatles remind us that life becomes increasingly miserable without the much-needed help from our friends. Try as we might, we can't do this on our own. We need support, acceptance, and friendship to get through the ups and downs of life. I want to encourage you, HSP, that you deserve these things, even if friendships have been bumpy or gone wayward for you in the past. Keep showing up, and ultimately, you, too, will get by with a little help from your friends.

JOURNAL PROMPTS

- *Reflect on a time when your friends avoided communicating their thoughts or desires with you. How did this experience make you feel? How did you handle the situation?*

- *Have you ever been in a situation where you felt you gave more than you received from your close friends? Describe the dynamics of that friendship. How did it impact your well-being? What steps can you take to create a balanced and healthy friendship?*

- *Think about a friendship that you consider authentic and meaningful. What qualities does this friendship possess? How do you feel? What actions do you and your friend take to nurture this friendship?*

- *Reflect on emotional intelligence (EQ) and its importance in forming healthy friendships. How does your EQ influence your behavior and relationships? How do you recognize and understand emotions in yourself and others? Write down an example of a situation where your emotional intelligence played a significant role in a friendship.*

ENRICHING ROMANTIC RELATIONSHIPS

"Having begun to love you, I love you forever – in all changes, in all disgraces, because you are yourself."

— THOMAS HARDY

In perhaps her most notorious work of fiction, *Wuthering Heights*, Emily Brontë introduces us to one of the most influential couples in literary history, Heathcliff and Catherine. At the risk of sharing any spoilers (though it was first published in 1847, so this is on you), the relationship between Heathcliff and Catherine is volatile at best. Raised together, their relationship becomes toxic and riddled with jealousy-fueled acts of antagonization. Their relationship aligns with the adage, "If I can't have them, no one can!" Catherine even goes so far as to haunt Heathcliff from her grave!

Despite the abuse and toxicity in their relationship, Catherine utters a phrase coined as wildly romantic in modern-day society:

> *"He is more myself than I am. Whatever our souls are made of, his and mine are the same."*

I've seen this quote in Instagram captions, on those shabby-chic chalkboards at weddings, and even stitched onto throw pillows. The more I turned this phrase over in my mind, though, the more I saw the connection between this line of thinking and highly sensitive people in relationships. People with sensory sensitivity are often tempted to merge with their significant other. Your partner's needs become your needs; your partner's hobbies become your hobbies, even though they might overwhelm your senses. This fusion of identities can often lead to relationship paralysis and emotional burnout, which may produce the opposite of its intended effect. Instead of being brought together by this identity fusion, the couple is pulled apart. Depending on the relationship, this fusion may result from several factors: in-authenticity in the relationship, a fear of confrontation or conflict, and the misunderstanding of one's self. Throughout the rest of this chapter, we'll parse out these different factors, giving you the tools to confidently and assuredly show up in your romantic relationships.

STRENGTHS OF HIGHLY SENSITIVE PEOPLE IN RELATIONSHIPS

According to researcher Dr. Karen Chenier, 36% of relationships are comprised of at least one highly sensitive person. Because of this percentage of partnered HSPs, we must describe what, exactly, an HSP looks like in a committed relationship.

According to Jenn Granneman, founder of the online community, *IntrovertDear*, HSPs are highly receptive to verbal and nonverbal communication, are more empathetic, prefer to avoid confrontation and engage in gentle conflict, and crave emotional intimacy.

Think, for a moment, about a previous or current relationship. *Do you see any of these patterns emerging?* Several of them are likely beneficial to both parties, but they can begin to fester if misconstrued or undercommunicated.

Let's unpack each of these aspects of an HSP in love:

Verbal and Nonverbal Communication
Pro: HSPs can easily interpret their partner's mood or emotions based on non-verbal cues. They are excellent active listeners who can often concisely paraphrase their partner's words for better clarity.
Con: HSPs may read too much into body language. They may also avoid sharing their feelings due to perceived negative body language or tone of voice.

Empathy
Pro: HSPs can easily put themselves in their partner's shoes to help them feel more understood and comforted.
Con: An HSP's empathetic nature may lead them to coddle their partner or accept toxic (or even abusive) behavior.

Conflict Avoidance and Gentle Communication
Pro: HSPs prefer to approach significant conversations more gently, reducing tension or potential hostility.
Con: An HSP's strict preference for conflict avoidance may cause them to show up inauthentically or simply avoid big conversations altogether, leading to resentment.

Emotional Intimacy

Pro: HSPs are professionals at creating and establishing safe and emotionally intimate scenarios and conversations.

Con: Because an HSP has a higher capacity for emotional intimacy, their constant desire for it may be perceived as emotional intensity and overwhelm their partner.

As you read through the aforementioned list, you may have been filled with any number of emotions or feelings (pride, shame, feeling understood). I want you to know that there are no wrong answers here. Perhaps as you perused the above pro and cons list, some unhealthy relationship patterns emerged, and you realized you have enacted them in your current or past relationships. Fear not, my friend, for it is possible to learn new patterns in your relationship, and the best news is that it all starts with you.

GETTING TO KNOW YOURSELF AND YOUR NEEDS

Alain de Botton, a British author and philosopher, wrote,

> "Do you love me enough that I may be weak

with you? Everyone loves strength, but do you love me for my weakness? That is the real test."

In terms of romantic relationships, I often used to believe that my sensory sensitivity was a weakness. I wanted to hide this part of myself because I was ashamed to let my partners see the "cons" of dating me. I didn't want to be perceived as melodramatic if we went out and the location and ambiance were too overwhelming. I was afraid to confront past partners about things that bothered me, and I was afraid to communicate what I needed from them to feel safe and loved. The good news is, after spending some time researching sensory sensitivity, I became more comfortable and proud of my tendencies, which meant I could foster healthier relationships.

Often, fellow HSPs have come to me stating that their partners seem to be taking advantage of their empathetic nature and go-with-the-flow attitude. Furthermore, HSPs often feel that their need to come down after over-arousal may cause their partner to be annoyed or irritated. According to Dr. Deborah Ward, HSPs may find themselves frequently attracting emotionally unhealthy or unavailable romantic partners. This is due to the "pros" listed above and an HSPs willingness to put others before themselves.

ENRICHING ROMANTIC RELATIONSHIPS   55

How, then, does an HSP forgo being used in romantic relationships? This is where it becomes crucial to establish practices that will help you get to know yourself and identify your needs in relationships. *First*, work on accepting your sensitivity. It is a part of you, and all of you, good and bad, strong and weak, are worthy of love. *Second*, remember the boundaries you established in Chapter 3; these will also help guide you in your romantic relationships. *Third*, remember you are not your partner's therapist, work on encouraging them to connect with a mental health professional.

Let's break these steps down into some action steps, shall we?

Step One
You are coming to terms with the fact that you're a highly sensitive young adult. You recognize that this is a little "different" than others. Still, you're happy to finally have begun doing the inner work. What are some ways you could continue to work toward accepting yourself?

1. Taking 1-2 minutes each morning to repeat affirmations. (Example: I am worthy of love and belonging) *For further help, check out my book on young adult affirmations entitled, "Empowered & Confident"!*

2. Working through journal prompts that help identify who you are and your preferences. (Example: A perfect day for me looks like…). *More journal prompts can be found at the end of this chapter.*
3. Attending therapy with a licensed professional to help you unearth your needs in a relationship

Step Two

You've established boundaries by identifying what's important to you in life. You're starting to brainstorm what you'd need from a romantic partner. Ask yourself these questions:

1. How will I communicate these boundaries to my partner?
2. How will we hold each other accountable if one of these boundaries is crossed?
3. What's important to me to make me feel safe and heard in a relationship?
4. What are some non-negotiables for you in a relationship?

Step Three:

Previously, we discussed setting boundaries for others but haven't yet discussed setting personal boundaries. Establishing personal boundaries will help you navigate relation-

ship foibles and promote healthy communication. Some healthy examples could be:

1. Practicing saying, "Honey, I'm here for you, and I love and support you. However, I don't have the tools to help you with this. Could we look into finding a therapist to work through this problem?
2. Taking time to unwind or "come down" by yourself each week (i.e., prioritizing reading time each week, taking a class without your partner, spending time with a friend or family member, etc.)

Implementing these changes to your communication methods may initially seem overwhelming (trust me, I've lived it!), but fret not, my fellow HSP, because I've seen these practices help my relationships and other peoples'. But, please know that it's not one size fits all. What works for me in my relationship may not work for yours.

COMMUNICATING YOUR NEEDS

Once, I heard a story about a mother who was backing her car out of the driveway. Looking one way over her shoulder, she asked her son if any cars were coming from the opposite direction. "No," he said calmly, "but there is a truck." In the same way, people in relationships often miscommunicate. We think our partner means one thing, but they're attempting to communicate another. If this happens during sensitive or weighty conversations, it may result in relational friction and dysfunction. This is particularly relevant for HSPs, who constantly seek verbal or non-verbal cues to their partner's emotional state to avoid conflict.

The road to resentment is paved with conflict avoidance and dysfunctional communication, which is why clinical psychologists Dr. John and Julie Gottman created the Gottman Method. The Gottman Method is a therapeutic tool that teaches couples "rules of engagement" for communication. By utilizing this method, couples mitigate negative communication and begin creating pathways for more profound emotional connection.

In her piece, *A Communication Tool Every HSP Needs to Learn,* psychotherapist Julie Bjelland, states that there are two people involved in Gottman method interactions: the Speaker and the Listener. By defining these roles, couples know that each will get a turn to speak and to listen. The Gottmans encourage the listener to take written notes of the speaker's thoughts to decrease tensions.

Each interaction is a formula, if you will, with the Speaker having three distinct roles:

1. State the problem using "I" statements.
2. Stick to the facts (i.e., don't try to interpret your partner's motives or thoughts)
3. Tell your partner what you need (use your "I" statements here, too)

The Listener has four parts to their role in this conversation:

1. Identify the speaker's story using active listening (i.e., "What I'm hearing from you is…")
2. Identify and validate the speaker's emotion(s) (i.e. "It makes sense that you feel…")
3. Define the speaker's positive need (i.e., "I'm hearing you need me to…)
4. Clarify (reiterate what you've discussed and make sure you're both on the same page)

Note: if you're unsure what your partner is feeling or can't identify their positive need, try asking them.

So, what would this look like played out? Let's look at a brief case study:

Cynthia and Felix have been married for a little under two years. Cynthia has noticed that Felix has spent the last 18 months prioritizing spending time with his friends. Cynthia wants Felix to be able to spend time with friends, but she wants to spend intentional one-on-one time with him, too. Cynthia decides she wishes to bring this to Felix's attention, so she asks if she can borrow some of his time the upcoming Sunday. At their meeting, Cynthia practices using "I" statements. Here's how it could play out:

> Cynthia: *I have noticed that we haven't been spending intentional time together lately, and it's making me feel like we're drifting apart. The story I'm telling myself is that you'd prefer to spend time exclusively with your friends rather than me. It would mean a lot to me if we could set aside some time each week, just you and me.*

> Felix: *What I'm hearing from you is that you're feeling sad because we haven't spent any intentional time together recently. It makes sense that you feel that way; now that I think of it, we haven't planned anything special recently. It sounds like you're positive need is to schedule more time together each week, is that right? Did I miss anything?*

Remember, we are all human, and conversations don't always go this seamlessly. Don't lose heart if it doesn't seem natural right away. Most of us were not taught how to properly communicate, and it's normal if there are some growing pains. The key aspect of the Gottman method is to listen intentionally without formulating a rebuttal. A healthy relationship comprises two people who actively desire to make the other feel seen and heard.

I want to note that the Gottman Method is not a substitute for couples therapy. If it's accessible and right for you, you may discuss this method with a couples therapist near you. Lastly, if you are in a relationship that frequently makes you feel emotionally or physically unsafe, please consider contacting a mental health professional specializing in treating those who have experienced domestic violence or call the Domestic Violence hotline.

TIPS FOR LOVING A HIGHLY SENSITIVE PERSON

If you're a partnered HSP, I recommend you let your partner know you're reading a chapter on flourishing romantic partnerships. It may even be helpful to have them read through this section specifically, as I'll address the finer points of loving an HSP in the following note. Ahem...

> Dear Lover of an HSP,
>
> Hi, I'm glad you're here. In the past few chapters, your HSP (highly sensitive person) and I have discovered exactly what it means to live as a sensory-sensitive person. As a brief synopsis: HSP's senses are magnified, which means they can easily experience sensory overload. As a lover of an HSP, this may mean you might need to slightly alter how you two navigate life together. Fret not, though, because to be with an HSP is often a wonderful experience.
>
> First, remember that the big things are the little things for an HSP. They don't need grand gestures (some of them may even loathe them), but their hearts will flutter if you remember their coffee order, pack an extra set of headphones in the event they forget theirs, or lovingly hug them tightly when they're overwhelmed.
>
> This intentionality is essential when communicating, as well. HSPs often take a while to identify their feelings because they're wading through all of the sensory stimuli around them. Practice giving them space and encouraging them to take time out if needed. Once they've identified what they're feeling, encourage them to share with you. After all, you're a safe person to them.
>
> Second, remember that HSPs are prone to overthink-

ing. Encourage them as they implement practices to help minimize the time they spend ruminating. Offer a listening ear when you're available, or encourage them to discuss their feelings in therapy.

Third, remember that they may be more sensitive to physical touch. This may mean they have a decreased pain tolerance. Remember, you're not expected to fix it, but it means a lot to them when you help alleviate their feelings. This sensitivity to physical touch also means the connection the two of you share is incredibly meaningful to them.

Lastly, know that your HSP will always be there with a listening ear. They will support you and will cherish their time with you. (And if you've made it this far, know that they are very pleased you're taking the time to learn more about them!)

Sincerely,
A Fellow HSP

WHERE DO WE GO FROM HERE?

In his critically acclaimed novel, *The Perks of Being a Wallflower*, Stephen Chbosky writes,

> "We accept the love we think we deserve."

I think this sentiment affects more relationships than we give it credit for, especially relationships in which HSPs are involved. Due to their differing needs, sensory-sensitive people often believe they are too much or demand outrageous acts from their loved ones. Because of this, they may shy away from voicing their own needs and may easily be trampled over in relationships, thus accepting the love they think they deserve.

The truth is every person everywhere has to develop a sense of self-love. It's an old and tried maxim, but it's true; we must accept ourselves before we can successfully love another. Each of us must flex our self-esteem muscles before we can truly be loved. I urge you to continue to get to know yourself and to spend time with yourself. Learn to appreciate your sensitivities as a gift rather than a curse. Remember, you are worthy of love and respect not despite your sensory sensitivity, but because of it. Sensory sensitivity should not be loved *around*; it shouldn't be avoided, but revered in a relationship. Look for a partner who sees this part of you and truly accepts and adores it. They're out there, I promise.

∽

JOURNAL PROMPTS

- *Reflect on your past or current relationships and identify any patterns of communication that align with the strengths of highly sensitive people. How have these patterns affected your relationships positively or negatively?*

- *Explore the concept of identity fusion in romantic relationships. Have you ever experienced a merging of identities with your partner? How did it impact your relationship? Reflect on the potential challenges and benefits of identity fusion for HSPs.*

- *Consider the concept of emotional intimacy in relationships. How do you define emotional intimacy, and how important is it to you? Reflect on your capacity for emotional intimacy and how it aligns with being highly sensitive.*

- *Reflect on your past or current relationship and consider the strengths and challenges that arise from being a highly sensitive person. Think about how your verbal and nonverbal communication, empathy, conflict avoidance, and desire for emotional intimacy have influenced your relationship dynamics. Are there any patterns or behaviors that you have noticed? How do these strengths and challenges impact your overall relationship satisfaction?*

CLAIMING CONTROL OF YOUR COLLEGE LIFE & LIVING SITUATION

"But your solitude will be a support and a home for you, even in the midst of very unfamiliar circumstances, and from it, you will find all your paths."

— RAINER MARIA RILKE

One morning during my Freshman year of college, I stumbled to the bathroom in the dorm I shared with my roommate. As I groggily approached the sink, I noticed what appeared to be either a small animal or a large dust bunny. Much to my dismay, I realized it was neither; it was human hair, pasted in large globs to the side of the sink. My roommate walked past in the hall with hair at least a foot shorter. He'd cut it because "it was getting too long, and it was too hot outside." I ended up having to ask him nicely to clean up the hair in the sink later that day.

Needless to say, living with people is hard, especially when you start as strangers, which is often the case for post-high school young adults. Take heed, I have good news; it is possible to take some semblance of control over the chaos that is college while respecting your sensory sensitivity.

If you're expecting a transition to college (or even a new living situation) soon, remember to take it easy on yourself. Transitions are difficult for everyone. This is especially true for HSPs, who take longer to adjust to their surroundings. It's okay if your sensory sensitivity is heightened due to the changes in your environment. You can implement certain practices or changes to help this transition go more smoothly, including: finding appropriate housing, creating a calming space, streamlining your schedule, and implementing healthy sleep and social boundaries. This chapter will teach us how to do these things and troubleshoot any perceived problem areas.

MAXIMIZING HOUSING OPPORTUNITIES & CREATING A CALMING SPACE

Samantha, a friend of mine, used to work at a small liberal arts college as a housing coordinator for incoming Freshmen. She was tasked with reading through roommate questionnaires to match students with potential roommates. She always got a laugh at the section titled "pet peeves," as she received many odd and seemingly random answers: "loud ukelele playing," wrote one. "I hate when couples sit in the same booth on dates," lamented another. While it gave her a chuckle, these responses often did not help her determine who would get along best as roommates.

When we move in with new people, it can be challenging to determine what we need for successful cohabitation. Our family of origin is our baseline for living amongst others, but our roommate's baseline differs. While we have different childhood experiences, many have not lived with non-relatives before entering college. Thankfully, there are several ways to navigate college successfully as an HSP.

As you begin to prepare for college, you will likely be approached by your university's housing department (this will look different at every university). Here, I encourage you to do two things: *answer any questions they provide truthfully* and *be outspoken about your needs.*

Genuinely answering any questions that will promote a better roommate match. For example, suppose you're not into roller derby. In that case, I recommend against listing it as one of your interests (even if it's something you think you'd *like* to try). It may be helpful to write down your interests and hobbies and brainstorm some of your living preferences. Doing so will help you when the time comes for you and your roommate to discuss boundaries.

Let's look at some examples (these questions may be helpful to ask yourself *and* your roommate):

- What do you spend your free time doing? What are your hobbies?
- When do you prefer to go to bed?
- Are you a morning person? A loud person? A heavy sleeper? A light sleeper?
- Are there any student groups you anticipate joining?
- Are you on the cleaner side or the messier side? How often do you clean?
- Are you an introvert or an extrovert? What times do you prefer people not to be in your space?
- What are your preferences for inviting guests over?

Your university will likely ask you if you need both academic and housing accommodations. I encourage you to discuss this with them before moving to campus. A good rule of thumb is to communicate your sensory sensitivity and *then* make your request. For instance, if you are overwhelmed by loud noises, you may want to avoid living at the center of campus due to your sensitivity and propensity to be overwhelmed by large groups of people. Don't be afraid to communicate this.

While being on the same page as your roommate will help make the transition to college living easier, there still may be a period of growing pains. You'll be tasked with learning to live in a dorm with significantly more people than you've likely previously experienced. There is usually more significant sensory stimulation in dorms because of this. Preparing for what's to come and making a game plan will likely help you grow accustomed to dorm life. Typically each dorm will have some sort of Resident Advisor (RA); try to meet with them early on to explain where you're coming from. They can help you brainstorm some ideas to help accommodate you (i.e., hall quiet time hours, dimming the hall lights, etc.).

Lastly, work to make a space that is comfortable for you. Most schools provide a bed, desk, dresser, and/or closet. Keep this in mind as you begin to buy items for dorm life. What do you like about living in your home now? What do you wish was improved? Work to create a space that's comforting to you. It may be you prefer a floor lamp to overhead lighting. Perhaps you get easily overstimulated by noises; maybe invest in some quality headphones or earplugs. (On a personal note, I would recommend getting a foam mattress topper.) By preparing your space, you create a haven to retreat to if the outside campus gets overwhelming.

Ok, so you've communicated your needs, set boundaries with your roommate, and set up your haven dorm; what next? I suggest brainstorming how you will navigate your need to "come down" in college. Sharing your school and/or work schedule with your roommate may be helpful. If they're comfortable with it, ask them to share theirs. This can help you identify times you will have exclusive access to the dorm. I recommend finding a spot or two elsewhere on campus when your dorm is unavailable. Perhaps you're a library person; see if you can find a comfy chair. If you prefer a coffee shop ambiance, try a few local ones. Lastly, remember, if it's accessible, it is sometimes helpful to leave campus to recharge and connect with the "outside world."

Take time and give yourself space to identify these new spots. As the semester progresses, you will likely fall into a routine, and campus life will become more familiar. If you are having trouble adjusting or if there are other big life things you'd like to talk about, most universities provide free counseling services to students. This will likely be on your university's website, or you can ask your RA. Lastly, if living on campus is not for you, that's okay. If you're able to live off campus or commute, those are excellent options are well. *You* get to decide your collegiate experience. The world is your oyster!

MANAGE YOUR SLEEPING AND SOCIAL METER

Much of your success in college will come down to your ability to use your time. Time management is helpful, and I'd recommend practicing it before moving to campus. In college, I preferred to block my time using my Google calendar. At the beginning of each semester, I would input my class times and schedule a 2-4 hour study time block a few days a week. Not only did this help me stay on task academically, but it also helped me identify my free time. When implemented, this practice allows for spontaneity with your free time while upholding personal responsibilities (i.e., work and school).

Perhaps the most manageable schedule to misman-age, though, is a sleep schedule, especially in college. It's easy to get caught up hanging out with friends or to begin to rely too heavily on pulling all-nighters to finish homework. Still, lack of sleep can be detrimental to your overall health. As an HSP, sleep deprivation will make it easier for you to become hyperaroused or burnt out. To support your long-term success at college, I highly recommend creating routines that help with a healthy sleep schedule. Determine the amount of sleep you need each night and set a reminder for when it's time to turn in. If you know you're going to be out late, try to get in a nap that afternoon. There's a lot of ebb and flow in college, so it's crucial to have personal boundaries.

Personal boundaries could look like this:

- The amount of time you'll do schoolwork each day
- The number of extracurriculars in which you'll participate
- How many nights a week you'll go out
- How many hours a week you'll work
- How many hours a day you'll sleep

Pick one of these boundaries to try to implement at a time. Over time, you will develop a routine supporting your experience in higher education as an HSP.

WHERE DO WE GO FROM HERE?

Over the years, many successful sitcoms have been made about the shenanigans of roommates (*Friends, New Girl, Big Bang Theory*). You'll notice a theme if you've watched any of these shows. Throughout every up and down, even through disagreements, the characters usually find their way back to each other to make amends. Obviously, those shows are scripted, but I think they often model roommate communication quite well. If two characters are fighting, they usually have a heart-to-heart at the end of the episode (after the entertaining shenanigans have ensued). Similarly, I encourage you to reach out to your roommate as you transition to a new living setting as a highly sensitive young adult. However, in real life, you will likely see more success if you forgo the sitcom shenanigans and are genuine at the start of an interaction.

It was Shakespeare who said,

"To thine own self be true,"

But he forgot to mention that, in order to be true to one's self, one must know themselves. I encourage you to identify the components of yourself (likes, dislikes, preferences, passions), so you can accurately share yourself with the new people you meet during young adulthood. Furthermore, to be true to one's self, you must hold yourself accountable. YOU are responsible for caring for yourself in adulthood, so it's vital to prioritize personalizing your collegiate experience as a highly sensitive young adult. Do this by learning to manage your time and creating a space that's unique to you! It will take some trial and error, but I encourage you to go forth, my friend, and prosper.

∼

JOURNAL PROMPTS

- *Reflect on your past experiences living with others or in shared living situations. How have these experiences shaped your preferences and needs regarding cohabitation? Consider any challenges you faced and what you learned from them.*

- *Imagine yourself in a new living situation, such as a college dorm or a shared apartment. Create a list of your living preferences, including factors like noise levels, cleanliness, personal space, and social boundaries. How would these preferences contribute to your overall well-being and comfort?*

- *Think about your current living space or a space you feel comfortable in. Describe the elements that make it calming and comforting to you. How can you recreate or incorporate these elements in your future living situation to create a haven for yourself?*

- *Consider the concept of personal boundaries and how they apply to your college life. Identify one aspect of your life (such as study time, extracurricular involvement, or socializing) where you can set a clear boundary for yourself. Describe how this boundary will benefit your well-being and help you navigate the challenges of college life as a highly sensitive young adult.*

PROSPER IN YOUR PROFESSIONAL LIFE

"If you don't like the road you're walking, start paving another one." - Dolly Parton

I still remember the day I "graduated" preschool because it was my first time getting stage fright. We donned our mini-graduation caps and gowns and, one by one, toddled to the front of the room so our teacher could prompt us on our favorite food, subject, and what we wanted to be when we grew up. I watched as each of my three-foot-tall classmates cheerfully bellowed things like "astronaut-ballerina!" or "fireman-veterinarian!"

Too soon, it was my turn, and I hadn't thought of a

future career! I mumbled about music and goldfish crackers, but when announcing my future vocation, I panicked. My palms started sweating, and my breath hitched. I looked up, my eyes pleading for my teacher's help.

"What about a doctor?" She asked.

"YES!" I vehemently agreed, even though the thought of blood made my skin crawl, and I had to look away when my mom stuck bandaids to my scraped knees. I'd agree to anything if it got everyone's attention off me and onto Michelle (who wanted to be a mommy and a mailman).

When it came time to graduate high school, my peers eagerly anticipated their future trades, but I was still on the fence. I picked something I enjoyed doing (music), but unlike my friends, I didn't have a clear-cut idea of how I'd use my degree in the future. Eventually, it worked itself out, and I became the tech director at a nonprofit. Still, it took some time for me to realize that there are specific work environments with which my sensory sensitivity is *incompatible.*

I sometimes wonder if my unwillingness to firmly determine a future career as an adolescent was due to my sensory sensitivity. Perhaps I was so focused on making my day-to-day environment livable that I didn't have it in me to prepare for my future. Perhaps you, too, have had difficulty landing on a career. Or, like some of my HSP friends, you picked a job only to realize you can't work in your chosen industry long-term. You may even be preparing for college or trade school and are unsure of which path to take. If so, I hope this chapter helps you identify your specific vocational needs as an HSP and boosts your confidence as you prepare to enter the workforce.

PROBLEMS THAT HIGHLY SENSITIVE PEOPLE FACE AT WORK

According to Andre Solo, a leading expert in sensory sensitivity and editor-in-chief of *Sensitive Refuge*, it is not uncommon for HSPs to struggle to identify a career, even though they are often competent and hardworking individuals. Often, there are several factors of specific careers that HSPs actively avoid, including fast-paced, loud, and physically demanding environments. As mentioned, this is not due to incompetence or drive, but sustainability. HSPs often struggle to tolerate intense environments for long periods of time. If subjected to demanding environments for too long, HSPs run the risk of burning out, thus significantly decreasing their quality of life, and causing them to become disconnected from other staff and teammates.

Furthermore, it is crucial to HSPs that their work matters. What matters to one HSP is different from another, but overall, HSPs often need to feel that they are contributing to society somehow. This may be why HSPs are prone to struggling in sales jobs, helping professions, and jobs that require conflict management and negotiation. To be clear, HSPs may very well be highly successful in the aforementioned professions, as they can quickly read others and identify others' preferences and desires. However, the need to constantly utilize their empathetic radar for potential sales, or for high-stakes confrontations, rapidly exhausts them.

It is not uncommon for HSPs to be perfectionists, either. This is true of both creative freelancers and nine-to-five warriors and, counterintuitively, may hinder workplace productivity. Because they are hyperaware of surrounding minutia, HSPs can hone in on specific details of processes or projects. This skill is both a blessing and a curse. It's a blessing because they often identify the problems or mistakes others miss. They are great troubleshooters and problem-solvers, which means they are invaluable to their more macro-oriented peers. It's a curse because their penchant for perfectionism often means HSPs struggle to see the forest for the trees. In other words, their attention to detail may slow them down.

Please note that *you* are the "master of your fate," as William Ernest Henly wrote in his 1875 poem, Invictus. You determine what career you're passionate about and wish to pursue. It is possible to be a highly-sensitive attorney or doctor. If it's something you care about deeply, know that I support you! If you have found yourself in an industry that exhausts you, but you cannot leave for the time being, let's discuss some ways you can cope (and maybe even succeed!).

BEING SUCCESSFUL ON YOUR OWN TERMS

Have you ever had a coworker that brags about constantly staying late at the office? Have you ever felt pressure to look busy so your boss thinks you're a hard worker? Have you ever been guilt-tripped when attempting to use your PTO? Society often programs us to think of success as the amount of work we accomplish or the overtime we're willing to invest in our jobs. This pressure can be so intense, people may find themselves competing to prove who works the hardest.

What if we reshaped this mentality? What if, instead of focusing on how much work we accomplish, we focused on how we felt while completing our work? Focusing on feeling over output is important for HSPs, who tend to prioritize productivity so their coworkers pay no heed to their sensitivities. You may be asking, how does one begin to prioritize how you feel completing work over accomplishments?

First, I encourage you to be selectively vulnerable

about your sensitivities. While there is no shame in being an HSP, not everyone is informed about sensory sensitivity. Begin with discussing your needs with HR, as they will be able to help you make the most out of the available accommodations. If your company doesn't have HR, look to identify emotionally mature people at your workplace. These are people who are typically open-minded and level-headed. This could be your supervisor, or it could be the person in the cubicle next to you. If you choose to disclose your sensitivity, it may be helpful to have someone who gets it. The following rule applies to most aspects of your personal life: *be careful who you share with at work.* Some people just won't get it, and that's okay.

Conversely, setting boundaries with your coworkers about what they share with you is also important. As an HSP, you run the risk of becoming a stand-in therapist for nearly everyone you meet. If you feel like someone is oversharing, it's okay to say, "I'm so sorry you're going through that, but I'm really not comfortable discussing it at work," or "I hear you, but, today, I'm just juggling a lot mentally. I recommend talking to our supervisor (or HR)."

If you find yourself in a supervisory position, remember to take time to care for your mental health. You are at an advantage as an empathetic HSP, so the good news is your subordinates will likely open up to you quickly. The bad news is they may begin to view you as their pseudo-therapist. My advice here is to know your resources. If your company provides Employee Assistance Programs (EAP), which often include assessment and therapy, financial advice, and other coaching services, take the time to help your staff enroll in the program. The key is to identify alternative supports for your team so the burden to care for them is not solely on your shoulders.

Next, spend some time personalizing your space. Whether you have an office or share a cubicle, it's crucial to feel peace of mind while working. After all, you'll likely be spending a significant amount of time in this space! If you're sensitive to overhead lights, invest in a lamp or two. (If you're in a shared area, talk to HR; they may be able to help you dim the overhead lights.) Are you always cold? Bring in a small blanket or large scarf to use. Or, if allowed, bring in a small space heater. If you're particularly sensitive to noise, invest in a small sound machine or listen to calming music. (Use headphones, though, don't be *that* person.) Last, add touches of home by including photos of loved ones or small, easy-to-maintain house plants. The more at peace and welcome you feel in your space, the happier you'll feel completing your work.

Lastly, and perhaps most obviously, I want to remind you to take breaks. Our society has programmed us to think we need to be in the trenches working the entirety of our 8-12 hour shift (and beyond). It's okay if you have a little downtime at work. In fact, taking breaks might even help you become *more* productive because it helps mitigate burnout and overwhelm. If it helps, you may even begin to schedule your day around your tasks.

A typical day at an office job might look like this:

>*9:00-11:00 a.m.: Work on projects or more demanding tasks first*
>
>*11:00-11:15 a.m.: Take a break (grab a coffee or walk around the office to say hi)*
>
>*11:15-12:00 p.m.: Read and respond to emails and voicemails*
>
>*12:00-1:00 p.m.: Leave your workspace for lunch!*
>
>*1:00-3:30 p.m.: Open time block for meetings*
>
>*3:30-3:45 p.m.: Take a break*
>
>*3:45-5:00 p.m.: Prep for tomorrow and/or learn something new*

Life can't be perfectly planned though, and you likely have a job more taxing and demanding than the above schedule, so I encourage you to start by beginning to schedule *one* 15-minute break into your day.

Over time, learning to take breaks will help you build stamina and increase workplace happiness.

NAVIGATING PERFORMANCE REVIEWS

One of the more daunting aspects of participating in the workforce is annual performance reviews. Performance reviews can be incredibly intimidating and uncomfortable, especially for HSPs, because sensory-sensitive brains tend to want to take things more personally. Julie Bjelland, a licensed psychotherapist who specializes in sensory sensitivity, states that this is due to HSPs' tendency to process the world using their "emotional" brain and not their "thinking" brain. Your emotional brain (also known as the limbic system) is how your brain processes sensory data. In contrast, your thinking brain (known as your cognitive system) is more logical and patterned-oriented. So, if you're an HSP in a performance review, your emotional brain will likely be in the driver's seat.

Taking perceived criticism to heart can be easy, so it's important to head into performance reviews with a few things in mind:

- We are *all* still learning.
- Each of us has room for growth.

- No one is mad at you (and if they are, they'll tell you).
- No one expects you to be perfect.
- A critique of your work is not a criticism of your character.

Lastly, remember you also are reviewing your work environment during your annual review. Now, don't let things build up over the year, but performance reviews are a good time for you to pitch ideas, discuss opportunities for growth (for you and your team), and discuss what you need to be more successful at your job.

POTENTIAL CAREERS FOR HIGHLY SENSITIVE YOUNG ADULTS

As you consider your future career or a career change, it is important to remember what we've learned about being an HSP in the workforce. Work to identify the type of environment that makes you most comfortable. Think about the people you want to work with: do you prefer to work as a group or individual? What type of field do you hope to be a part of? Technology? Healthcare?

Suppose you've thought all these questions through but still have difficulty determining a specific career.

In that case, I've compiled a (non-inclusive) list of potential careers for HSPs:

- Creative arts/freelancing (i.e., journalism, editing, graphic design, photography, coding)
- Helping professions (i.e., Social services/work, clinical mental health, nursing, direct care)
- Teaching, being an adjunct professor, or teaching English as a second language
- Environmental/climate care (Department of Natural Resources, animal shelters, conservation)
- Librarian/bookstore clerk
- Personal fitness instructor (yoga teacher, physical therapist)

WHERE DO WE GO FROM HERE?

If you pick a future career randomly whenever someone asks you what you want to be when you grow up, know that you're not alone. Many adults still don't know. In fact, more people than you think struggle to identify an appropriate career. If you're one of them, take your time, ask questions, and do your research. If you pick a career and decide it's not for you after a few years, know that this is totally normal! Younger generations tend to have more job experience than their predecessors, who more often stayed at employers for significant periods (even their entire careers).

Remember, it's okay to change your mind.

Building a successful career as an HSP mainly relies on your self-awareness and advocacy. Once you know what you need from your work environment, you can better communicate with the powers that be. You'll also be able to personalize your workspace, leading to workplace happiness and helping add to your quality of life. Lastly, remember you're young, and it's okay to make mistakes! You have many opportunities before you, and YOU get to decide what to do with those opportunities.

JOURNAL PROMPTS

- *Reflect on your past experiences and the career paths you have considered. Have you ever felt pressured to choose a specific career based on societal expectations or the influence of others? How did that make you feel, and how did it impact your decision-making process?*

- *Consider the work environments that make you feel most comfortable and productive. Are any specific factors, such as noise levels, pace, or physical demands, significantly affecting your well-being in a work setting? How can you prioritize these factors when exploring potential career options?*

- *Explore your own definition of success in the workplace. How do you measure your success, and how does society influence these perceptions? How can you shift your focus from solely accomplishing tasks to prioritizing your well-being and how you feel while completing your work?*

- *Think about your experiences with performance reviews or evaluations. How do you typically react to feedback or critiques of your work? Are there any strategies you can employ to better navigate these situations as an HSP, keeping in mind that reviews of your work do not reflect your worth as an individual?*

SQUASH SOCIAL MEDIA OVERWHELM

❦

"The secret of life is enjoying the passage of time."

— JAMES TAYLOR

Okay, *I can do this. It's not even that serious.* I thought this to myself as I watched the square icons on my iPhone's home screen wiggle. My thumb hovered over the quivering Instagram app, and I hastily deleted it, followed by TikTok and Facebook while I still had momentum. You see, a few months before I started writing this book, I decided to take a six-month social media hiatus. I'd had a rough couple of months leading up to this decision; I was burnt out, depressed, and overwhelmed by the thought of a simple click to a social media app rendering me the unfortunate recipient of an onslaught of global, panic-inducing news. On top of that, my self-esteem took a nosedive every time I opened an app and saw one of my "friends" posting a life update. I often compared their promotions, engagements, and perceived success to my lack thereof.

Why am I falling so far behind? I'd think to myself. *And how will I create a decent quality of life when the world is so messed up?*

This line of thinking would lead me down one of two pathways. I'd either spend hours researching how to "better myself," thus creating a false sense of productivity, leading to burnout. Or, I'd fall into the depths of nihilistic despair. Who cares, right? The world is in shambles! Eventually, I found myself staring at my wiggling apps, hoping some time away would help me cope with the large amount of anxiety-inducing information I had allowed my brain to entertain.

You may have noticed a similar pattern in your life. Have you noticed that the amount of screen time you accrue each week is comparable to a part or full-time job? Do you spend time doom-scrolling or comparing your livelihood to Hollywood's elite? Have you noticed you've been down on yourself about your appearance or productivity more often? These questions indicate someone who's spent much time perusing social media.

Don't get me wrong; social media can be used for good. We love watching videos of dogs being adopted or veterans being united with their children in airports. Social media can be used to promote social good, invite people to community events, and even meet your significant partner. But, one wrong click and an algorithm will make you wonder how you ended up where you did.

This is especially prevalent for HSPs, whose levels of empathy and proclivity to overstimulation make them excellent victims for social media algorithms to prey upon. Throughout this chapter, we will examine how unrestricted social media use harms HSPs, how to avoid doom-scrolling and news overload, and how to engage with it simply and mindfully.

HOW SOCIAL MEDIA HARMS THE HIGHLY SENSITIVE

In the Fall of 2021, *The Wallstreet Journal* published an article revealing documentation that suggests there is significant data that Instagram (owned by Facebook) is detrimental to the mental health of teenage girls. This claim was quickly downplayed and repudiated by the powers that be at Facebook. Still, the public met the article with a loud and resounding: "Yeah, man, we know."

I saw this article shared by those I follow on my own social media (the irony of which was not lost on me). We all subconsciously know that we spend large amounts of time comparing our lives to those we see on the internet, whether it is people we know IRL or our favorite parasocial relationships. This constant comparison is often the catalyst for negative thinking.

Social media is meant to be addictively stimulating, which is why so many people have a hard time logging off. This is especially tricky for HSPs, who may find themselves "addicted" to scrolling through social media, but exhausted from the constant overstimulation. This overstimulation can be the precursor for mental and physical illness and dysregulation. According to the JED Foundation, an organization dedicated to the betterment of adolescent mental health, young people who use social media may experience an increase in depressive symptoms, negative perception of self, and even the exacerbation of eating disorders. Unfortunately, teens and young adults are the most susceptible to the adverse side effects of social media usage.

Furthermore, as HSPs, we run the risk of inducing an "emotional hangover." The ability to quickly and easily empathize with the plight of others means HSPs are depleting emotional and mental energy with each scroll. This means our constant online emotional availability lends itself to emotional unavailability in real life. It also means that the ever-constant access to global news and pandemonium allows HSPs to be more easily blitz tackled with horrifying news, which is often not easy for sensory-sensitive people to shake.

EXPERIENCING NEWS OVERLOAD

I started following the news after college when I believed that being a "real adult" meant knowing all the terrible things happening in the world. I know this sounds pessimistic, but the constant barrage of gut-wrenching information relayed to me via TV, radio, and articles was enough to render anyone mute or cause a serious psychological implosion.

Since the dawn of time, news media consumption has evolved globally. Our first ancestors communicated information orally, through anecdotes and songs. In the early 1600s, the first newspapers emerged in Europe, which made organized information more accessible to those who could read. In 1844, Samuel Morse introduced the world to the telegraph, which allowed people to communicate previously unprecedented distances in a faster amount of time. By the 1960s, the world was tuning into FM radio programming for broadcasts. The 1970s saw the genesis of both Microsoft and Apple

Computers, Inc. In 1980, *The Columbus Dispatch* (est. 1871) became the first online news publication. Then, in 1991, the world forever changed when Sir Timothy John Berners-Lee invented the World Wide Web. Media had come so far. By 2001, the entire world tuned in to watch the attacks on the World Trade Center. By the 2010s, journalists and private citizens were recording news media on their iPhones. Today, the global population has access to previously unequaled amounts of information. For instance, in February of 2022, my friends and I watched in horror as private citizens posted TikToks of Ukraine being invaded by Russian forces. Had we just witnessed the commencement of World War III over a dance app?

When you think about it, this constant availability of news means that a person could quite literally spend all of their waking hours being inundated with newly released headlines and would still wake up "out of the know" the following day. I'd be lying to you if I said I didn't struggle to balance staying well-informed and the drinking-from-a-fire-hose feeling the 24/7 news cycle instills. However, after a few years of practice, I now have some tricks to avoid news overload.

Below are a few of the strategies I've implemented:

Make it Bite Sized

As mentioned before, constantly receiving news may lead to some serious anxiety symptoms and feelings of impending doom. Instead of spending hours pursuing headlines or watching your favorite news anchor share breaking news, you could try reducing your news intake. Your nervous system will thank you. Try to cut back to 10-15 minutes of news intake daily. Go into this time with a game plan of how to cope with news you find overwhelming. Try taking a few deep breaths, acknowledging your feelings, and accepting that it's okay to feel that way. Instead of heading to an online newspaper or watching clips, reading through a daily newsletter like Morning Brew or The Skimm may also be helpful.

Say Goodbye to Negative Feeds

Don't let your Aunt Meryl's obsession with bad news become your own. Whether you agree with her politically or not, if Aunt Meryl is *only* posting bad news, it will also tempt you to fall into a doom spiral. Likewise, scroll through the people you follow on Instagram; which influencers make you feel like reheated garbage? Unfollow them! It doesn't have to be forever, but taking a break from those with seemingly perfect and unattainable lives will do wonders for your mental health!

Prepare Downtime Activities

Perhaps the greatest instigator of our endless scrolling is our lack of preparation regarding what to do with our downtime. It sounds counterintuitive to plan to relax, right? However, establishing a game plan will help you avoid coming to from a TikTok doomscroll at 1 AM, only to realize you haven't eaten dinner and need to work the next day. You can schedule downtime using the settings in your phone or leave your phone to charge in another room. Okay, so you've put your phone on do not disturb, what now? Spend some time identifying a new hobby. You could read, meet up with a friend, garden, cook; the list goes on!

Slowly, and with practice, you will start to feel more at ease with the world in which you're living. By reducing your time spent reviewing horrible headlines, watching live streams from awful situations, and reading political hot takes, your peace of mind will once again return to you. Remember, it is important to be well-informed, but it is not imperative to miss out on your life to do so.

USING SOCIAL MEDIA IN A HEALTHY MANNER

Similar practices may be implemented to better encourage healthy social media usage in your life. All too often, we get comfortable living our lives "online." We do things for the 'Gram or post a story and continuously check to see who's watched it. We see people with the bodies or belongings we want and fall into a pattern of self-loathing. I know I've fallen into these traps before, and it's okay if it takes time to remodel your relationship with social media. Similarly to our other relationships, our relationship with social media needs to have healthy boundaries established, lest it infringes on our one precious life and takes much more than we are really willing to give. What would it look like to be in control of your social media use instead of being controlled by it?

First, begin to practice taking everything with a grain of salt. Those photos you see of Kylie Jenner and Beyonce? They're photoshopped, my friend. That influencer that is promoting special diet tea on their Instagram? Yeah, they're sponsored and probably don't even drink it. The next time you peruse social media, try to remember this practice. Most things on the internet have been enhanced, so let yourself off the hook! If they're not perfect, you don't have to be either. Instead of following picture-perfect influencers, follow people and accounts that make you feel represented or better about yourself.

Next, as mentioned before, practice limiting your screen time. You could have a friend set the password for your screen time limits; that way, you can't just throw in the password you created and keep scrolling. It also may be helpful to turn off push notifications for social media apps so you're not risking a 2-hour scroll when you open the app to check your notification.

Lastly, take time to practice being thankful for what you have. By implementing gratitude, you rewire your brain to see life's positives. You'll become a natural at identifying the little things in life that bring you peace or joy. When you remove time spent on your phone, add time to stop and smell the roses. This can be done by practicing living slowly and mindfully. When we practice mindfulness, we make the cognitive and intentional decision to be present in our lives.

PRACTICING MINDFULNESS

The first example of practicing mindfulness is a rapidly expanding practice that's actually been around for thousands of years: meditation. I know, I know. You're probably thinking, "Jordan, I'm not some Buddhist monk, and I don't have hours to devote every day to sitting and thinking about trying not to think about thinking!" Needless to say, I understand any skepticism. The beautiful thing about meditation is that it means something different to everyone. For some, it's a deeply spiritual practice that helps them connect with their higher power. For others, it helps them cope with the turbulence of day-to-day stressors. Meditation, for me, is a pillar of mindfulness because it reminds me to take a deep breath and be in the moment. This practice then transcends into my daily life. Not only does meditation help you manage your stress, but you will also learn to acknowledge and accept negative emotions (a skill many of us are never taught). You may even be able to start to tolerate that overbearing coworker that refuses to work in silence. Your physical body may see improvements, too. Your blood pressure may be lowered, you'll likely be able to sleep better, and you'll be better equipped to deal with any chronic illness.

There are many ways to practice meditation. Perhaps the most accessible and approachable is guided meditation. While practicing guided meditation, you may spend time envisioning goals, and your favorite, most comforting places, while noticing the world using your five senses. You could also choose to practice mindfulness meditation, in which you spend time identifying and focusing on the present moment. Thoughts may come to you, but you learn to accept them and let them go. You might even try yoga, which is a sort of meditative movement. Sometimes, moving can help us focus on the present moment rather than worrying about life's stressors. Spend some time identifying what sounds most interesting to you, and give it a shot!

Speaking of moving, another way to practice mindfulness is to work some type of movement into your day. I'm not saying you must pick up CrossFit or run a marathon, but spending time moving your body in a way you enjoy will help you gain mental clarity and many other benefits.

According to Harvard Medical School, implementing regular aerobic exercise helps prepare your body for future physiological symptoms of stress. This means the next time your body wants to go into sensory-sensitive overload, you'll have a built-up physiological tolerance to stress and a higher capacity for new environments or experiences. Similarly, incorporating aerobic exercise into your daily life may help you cope with symptoms of anxiety or depression. Have you ever been feeling down and realized your body feels more lethargic and you're moving more slowly? Conversely, decidedly choosing to exercise will likely help your brain start to feel a little better, too.

If you decide to exercise, moving that exercise outside may reap further benefits. According to Dr. Lacie Parker, "Nature is the ultimate 'release valve' for overstimulated HSPs." When you're someone with sensory sensitivity, most locations feel cataclysmic. In nature, though, HSPs can gently absorb the surrounding world without their senses being overstimulated. For me, I feel most at peace walking through the woods and taking in the musky smell of the sturdy evergreens. I love taking in the crunch of pine needles under my feet and the chime of birdsong. You see, when 2020 introduced us to a global pandemic, I started going outside (strictly because there was little else to do). I thought I would get too hot, or hungry, or tire too easily, and sometimes that was true.

From these escapades, I learned that I find nature deeply healing. The trees will always be there, quietly reaching up and up. Brooks will continue to dance over riverbeds, even while no human eye is there to appreciate their beauty. Deer will continue to bound across the forest floor, squirrels will flick their tails, and leaves will continue to fall, all without a care in the world. It is what they are meant to do, so they do it. Nature is not motivated by productivity, money, or power; it simply is. This is an excellent reminder for HSPs: it is okay to live a quiet life, simply doing what makes you feel like *you*, and for no one's happiness but your own. That, in itself, is what it means to be mindful.

WHERE DO WE GO FROM HERE?

In the spring of 1977, singer-songwriter James Taylor penned his song, Secret O' Life, at his home in Martha's Vineyard. In it, Taylor serenades his audience with the idea that the meaning of life is living in the moment. This is why I chose to open this chapter with a lyric from the song: "The secret of life is enjoying the passage of time." There is no right or wrong way to enjoy the passage of time; only the act of doing it matters. I often think HSPs feel they're missing out on life because they don't live their lives like others do. They keep less company and prefer serenity to big, sprawling cities or events. Being an HSP sometimes means taking more frequent daily breaks than others. There is nothing wrong with this or with you.

You get to decide how you pass your time, and, as we've seen throughout this chapter, you have many options. You could spend it scrolling through social media for hours on end. You could spend it constantly absorbing all the bad news in the world. You might even choose to do both. There is an alternative option, though. It is living slowly, enjoying the good moments, and accepting the bad. You get to build your own life, and I encourage you to fill it with practices that allow your sensory sensitivity to shine. You have been given a gift as an HSP because you have an unprecedented capacity for mindfulness.

Lastly, I'll leave you with this: When asked about the title of his song, James Taylor stated that he decided to forgo the title "Secret of Life" because, to him, it felt too pretentious. Instead, he chose to stick with "Secret O' Life, " a nod to Pep O Mint and Wint O Mint, popular candies at the time. He liked the irreverence, and I think I do, too. *After all, it's not that serious.*

JOURNAL PROMPTS

- *Reflect on your social media usage and its impact on your mental health. How often do you compare your life to others on social media? How does this comparison affect your self-esteem and overall well-being?*

- *Consider the strategies mentioned in the section for avoiding news overload. How do you currently consume news and do you feel overwhelmed by the constant barrage of information? How might implementing the suggestions in the chapter, such as limiting news intake and saying goodbye to negative influences, help improve your mental state?*

- *Explore your relationship with social media and the boundaries you have established. Are you in control of your social media use, or does it control you? How might you practice taking everything on social media with a grain of salt and focusing on accounts that make you feel represented or positive about yourself?*

- *Contemplate the concept of mindfulness and its potential benefits for your well-being. How often do you live in the present moment and appreciate the little things in life? Have you tried any mindfulness practices, such as meditation or movement, and how have they affected your overall mindset and stress levels?*

EXPERIENCING THE MIND-BODY CONNECTION

The mind moves the body, and the body follows the mind.

— H.E. DAVY

Disclaimer: I am not a healthcare professional. We all have individual healthcare needs; before making any major lifestyle changes, discuss them with your primary care physician.

I enjoy several simple pleasures in life: sleeping in, watching the sunset, spending time with friends, and, most importantly, tucking into some greasy and comforting Taco Bell. You can imagine my dismay when I realized my love of spicy and flavorful food started negatively impacting my digestive system, and consuming these types of food led to severe stomach pain, constipation, and food-aversion anxiety. My doctor ran several tests, but ultimately, we were still left with a big fat question mark. There seemed to be nothing "wrong" with me, even though my irritated bowels upended my life.

During this time, I was also going through some major life stressors. My then-girlfriend and I had decided to go our separate ways permanently. Ours had been a tumultuous relationship often indicative of two people in their late teens and early twenties. In the five years we dated, we had broken up and gotten back together several times. This constant oscillation of emotions was starting to impact my mental and physical health significantly. The post-break-up chalupas lead to heartburn and stabbing abdominal pain. This pain led to feelings of depression and anxiety which I then chose to soothe with a Crunchwrap Supreme. Thus, the gassy cycle continued.

Finally, after some research and direction from my

doctor, I realized there may be a connection between what I felt emotionally and how my body felt physically. Even more, my emotional state was highly impacted due to my sensory sensitivity. This means that when I felt sad, I felt *really* sad, and my body was significantly influenced. Perhaps you have a similar story: unexplained chest pains or heart palpitations? Severe nausea? Migraines or headaches? These can all be symptoms of emotional exhaustion or even distress. Throughout this chapter, we'll unpack the mind-body connection and just how an HSP might learn to care for their mental and physical health.

HARMFUL THOUGHT PATTERNS AND COGNITIVE DISTORTIONS

Cognitive distortions are illogical or impractical thought patterns many of us fall victim to. HSPs, especially, find themselves tempted to fall into cognitive distortions. These distortions are that gnawing, ever-present feeling of anxiousness and worry; the idea that if something can go wrong, it will. Each of us is affected differently by cognitive distortions, but, over time, this constant distorted thinking can result in some pretty life-altering physiological symptoms for us all.

Cognitive distortions can be comprised of several combinations of thought patterns. You may consistently return to one thought pattern or build upon others. No matter what, cognitive distortions can seriously affect your quality of life.

Let's take a look at some common cognitive distortions:

Catastrophizing

As mentioned earlier, you may fall into this thought pattern if your motto is: "If something can go wrong, it will." Should you find this to be accurate, you likely struggle with catastrophizing. People who catastrophize tend to see only the worst in situations. They may also tend to magnify poor situations allowing them to conjure up some pretty terrible "what if" situations.

Personalization

Do you tend to take the blame (even when unwarranted) just to keep the peace? Do you assume that you're the villain in every disagreement? If so, you may struggle with personalization. Those who struggle with personalization often disproportionately blame themselves when something goes wrong in another's life.

Mental Filtering

Those who fall victim to mental filtering tend to see the glass as half empty instead of half full. They tend to remember events that made them feel negative emotions while "filtering" out the positive ones.

It can be challenging to navigate the labyrinth that is cognitive distortion. Being trapped thinking the worst of yourself or your situation can take a toll on your psyche. Learning to reframe your perceptions and thought processes is no easy task. Still, it can ultimately help encourage a better quality of life. Once you can identify negative thoughts more quickly, you will be the master of them.

One way you can begin to take control of your cognitive distortions is to write them down. My therapist taught me this trick a few years ago, and it has been a practice I've returned to whenever I start to feel like I'm back in the labyrinth. Set a time of day that works for you to sit down with a pen and paper to list all your negative thoughts. I called this my "anxiety time." Throughout the day, whenever I was tempted by a cognitive distortion, I would think, "Nope, not time to be anxious yet; I'll have to wait until my nightly anxiety time."

A typical anxiety time list might look like this:

- What if I never land a promising career?
- What if Suzy thinks I'm a jerk because I didn't smile at her widely enough?
- What if all my friends secretly hate me because I asked them to pay their share of the Airbnb in Cancun?

Essentially, anxiety time is a time to get out all of your "what-if" questions. As a bonus, you can answer these questions using a healthier framework:

What if I never land a promising career?

Answer: My worth is not tied to my career; I enjoy my babysitting job right now.

What if Suzy thinks I'm a jerk because I didn't smile at her widely enough?

Answer: Suzy probably didn't think anything of that interaction and went on her merry way. Besides, it's none of my business what Suzy thinks of me!

What if all my friends secretly hate me because I asked them to pay their share of the Airbnb in Cancun?

<u>Answer</u>: My friends care about me; if they ever really have a problem with me, I trust they'll tell me. Reminding them that they owe their share of the Airbnb is okay.

It may seem awkward initially, but after a few sessions, your brain will reframe your thoughts in real-time. So when you think you've offended Suzy at the office, you can immediately talk yourself out of your distortion. It also means you won't spend the whole day ruminating, just during the 15 minutes it takes you to write your list.

THE MIND-BODY CONNECTION

You may have heard it said that the eyes are the windows to the soul. Similarly, the body can be a window to the mind. A mind-body connection is the fusion of thoughts, feelings, and physiological symptoms. Perhaps you have been emotionally distraught during a breakup and have been met with deep, aching pains in your chest. Maybe you've been nauseous after a disagreement with a friend or family member. We often aren't taught it in health class, but our day-to-day emotions significantly impact our physical well-being.

Your brain communicates with your body by utilizing neuropathways composed of neurotransmitters, hormones, and chemicals that control every one of your bodily functions. Specifically, your emotional cortex (composed of the amygdala, hippocampus, and pre-frontal cortex) is the part of your brain that, you guessed it, controls your emotions and emotional responses. Furthermore, your amygdala controls your parasympathetic nervous system, which is responsible for your flight, fight, or freeze response. Your body initiates these responses to keep you alive.

Suppose you are a person with a brain prone to cognitive distortions. In that case, you may feel like you're repeatedly engaging your parasympathetic nervous system. When you constantly feel like you're living in a life-or-death situation, your body will react as such. This may lead to some uncomfortable physiological symptoms, like stomach aches, migraines, or heart palpitations.

This is what was happening to me after my break up. My sadness and loss were causing my brain to tell my body something was wrong. From there, my body struggled to digest Taco Bell and then other less spicy foods. My chest ached from feeling so heartbroken. I learned that, especially as an HSP, I had to be more careful about how I treated my body as I healed.

The central aspect of healing I discussed with my doctor was my diet. He informed me that, overall, our food choices do have an impact on how we feel. As a man in his early twenties who practically lived off fast food, this was a hard pill to swallow. Unfortunately, man cannot live off Little Caesers alone. Slowly but surely, I started making minor changes to my diet and noticed some relief. I also reduced my drinking significantly because alcohol was tearing up my stomach. I noticed that it was making me feel bloated and inflamed.

It can be challenging to determine which foods are negatively affecting your body. By eliminating certain foods (under the guidance of my doctor), I started to notice my life was less interrupted by IBS symptoms. My doctor and I also discussed a temporary Low FODMAP diet. According to Monash University, FODMAPs are different sugars your body struggles to digest. When your body struggles to digest these foods, they aren't properly absorbed by your intestines. When high FODMAP foods hit your small intestine, they meet the first of many roadblocks. Because these foods move so slowly through your digestive tract, they absorb significant amounts of water, allowing the food to ferment by the time it meets your large intestine.

This fermentation creates a considerable amount of gas and, when combined with the excess water, causes your intestines to expand, making life a whole lot more uncomfortable. This expansion often causes that stabbing feeling in your gut.

Studies have shown that temporarily decreasing your intake of high FODMAP foods may significantly alleviate any IBS symptoms.

It becomes imperative, then, that we unpack what sugars make up the acronym FODMAP, so they can be avoided:

>FERMENTABLE - Carbohydrates that become fermented in your gut, leading to increased gas.

>OLIGOSACCHARIDES - Fructans and GOS is found in foods like wheat, barley, and onions.

>DISACCHARIDES - Lactose is found in foods like milk, yogurt, and ice cream.

>MONOSACCHARIDES - Fructose is found in foods like honey, apples, and high-fructose corn syrup.

>AND

>POLYOLS - Foods that consist of added sugars or

are high in sugars, like honey, agave, and peaches.

IF THIS RESONATES WITH YOU, it may be beneficial for you to reach out to your doctor. After you've discussed a low FODMAP diet with them, you can download a list of Low FODMAP foods on Monarch University's website. Typically, the low FODMAP diet is best utilized by implementing three phases: elimination, reintroduction, and customization. By eliminating high-FODMAP foods, you give your body time to heal and give your system some rest. By slowly re-introducing foods, you can better identify which foods make you feel worse and what quantities of high FODMAP foods your body can handle. By customizing, you can finalize which foods don't disturb your digestive system. It may be different for you than others, which is why this step is essential.

Furthermore, according to the Food for the Brain Foundation, there does appear to be a link between leaky gut and mental health. When you ingest food your body struggles to digest, your gut will develop an unhealthy microbiome, leading to a leaky gut. Leaky gut is characterized by increased permeability in your intestines, meaning all those nutrients can pass through your intestines and to your bloodstream, thus causing inflammation. According to a 2015 study published in the National Library of Medicine, researchers have identified significant links between the gut microbiome and the central nervous system, thus indicating what you put in your body may affect your mental health.

I was able to alleviate some of my symptoms of IBS and depression by restructuring my diet. Suppose you feel bloated or inflamed and are also experiencing symptoms of depression and anxiety. In that case, discussing what you've learned with your healthcare provider may be helpful. In addition, you may find that your body lacks certain vitamins and minerals, which may also affect your mental and physical health. For instance, studies have shown that insufficient levels of B6 in your body may make you more susceptible to symptoms of depression. B vitamins play several roles, including strengthening immunity and balancing your hormones. Interestingly, B vitamins are produced in your gut. Now, before you blindly supplement, it should be noted that many vitamins can be incorporated into your diet via foods. For instance, if you discover you lack B6, you may supplement by incorporating more chicken, peas, fish, etc., into your diet.

WHERE DO WE GO FROM HERE?

Suppose I have learned anything about creating a healthy mind-body connection. In that case, one must take a holistic approach when addressing physical and mental health. However, I genuinely believe this looks different for each of us. For me, it was cleaning up my diet and ensuring I ate enough quality, nutrient-dense foods. For you, it could be practicing meditation, as mentioned in the previous chapter, or implementing an exercise routine. For others, it could be scheduling some downtime to do something they want to do instead of running around completing their seemingly never-ending list of should-dos.

When taking a holistic approach, it's important to remember that the body and the mind are interconnected. Anything you do to or with your body will affect your mind and vice versa. As an HSP, it is even more imperative that you recognize this link, as your body may be triggered more easily than non-HSPs. Prioritizing your physical health means attending annual checkups, addressing nutritional needs, sleeping, and moving. After implementing these things into your routine, you'll notice how your body and mind feel if you forgo one of your practices. For instance, if you stay up too late a few nights in a row, you'll notice it will make you feel groggier and might exacerbate any depressive symptoms.

Prioritizing your physical well-being is an act of self-care, especially for someone who is easily overstimulated. We'll go into self-care more in the next chapter, but I want to leave you with this: the mind-body connection is a tool to be utilized. It can be overwhelming to think of everything you "should" do to improve this connection, or to consider all the things you'll have to remove to enhance your mind-body connection. I want to urge you to avoid falling into this line of thinking. Instead, think of one thing you might add to your daily life to make you feel a little better. For instance, you could schedule an appointment with your doctor to discuss what you've learned in this chapter (it counts!). Lastly, remember you'll still be able to partake in life's simple pleasures (I still get fast food occasionally). Taco Bell still has my heart; it just doesn't have my gut, too.

JOURNAL PROMPTS

- Reflect on a time when you experienced a strong mind-body connection. Describe the emotions you were feeling and the physical symptoms that accompanied them. How did this experience affect your overall well-being?

- Consider your own thought patterns and cognitive distortions. Are there any recurring negative thoughts or beliefs you tend to fall into? Write them down and explore how they might be impacting your mental and physical health.

- Have you ever practiced writing down your negative thoughts and reframing them? If not, give it a try. Set aside a specific time of day to list your negative thoughts and then provide healthier alternatives or perspectives. How does this exercise make you feel?

- Explore the potential impact of your diet on your mental and physical health. Are there any specific foods or food groups you suspect might negatively affect you? Consider discussing this with a healthcare provider and researching dietary *approaches, such as the low FODMAP diet mentioned in the chapter. Reflect on any changes you could make to improve your well-being.*

EMBRACING SELF-CARE

"Taking care of myself doesn't mean 'me first,' it means, 'me, too.'"

— L.R. KNOST

In December 2020, as the snow was piling up in mid-Michigan, I was once again drowning in a storm of overwhelm and burnout. As mentioned in the previous chapter, I was navigating severe symptoms of IBS, a tumultuous relationship, the culmination of an intense personal project with a strict deadline, and several yuletide events for which I was responsible. My daily routine consisted of consuming copious cups of coffee (even though my gut hated me for it), moving with a zombie-like gait, trying to find the emotional capacity to have a relationship with my then-girlfriend, and crashing which hopes of getting 4-5 hours of sleep (on a good day).

Even though I felt I would emotionally crack, I had no idea how to fix it. Prioritization of self-care was a foreign concept, and the thought of expending my energy to care for myself sounded daunting. Each time I tried to research self-care, I was met with strict "dos" and "don'ts." I didn't realize that my time spent taking care of myself was something I got to craft on my own.

Perhaps you're at your wit's end. Maybe you're still subscribing to "hustle culture." Hustle culture, popularized in the 2010s, is a practice of prioritizing work and the expenditure of physical and mental resources to "optimize" productivity. It meant getting to work early, skipping lunch, and staying late or working a double. It meant missing your child's karate matches and dinner with your loved ones. They chanted to themselves, "Rise and grind, rise and grind," in an effort to mentally push through their exhaustion. We were sold a lie that this was the *American Dream*. But the problem is, when you prioritize productivity, you under-value self-care. Think of it like gas in a car: once your tank is empty, you're not going anywhere! You can't expect to go on a cross-country road trip on fumes.

If my burnout story resonates with you, know there are ways to begin enjoying your life again. I know choosing to prioritize yourself and your life outside of work may cause you to feel guilty or ashamed, but I think it's important to remember that you're working to live. Your job is a building block; a tool you use to build the life you want.

HSPs, especially, need help navigating hustle culture. With limited energy, they succumb to burnout more quickly than their non-sensitive peers. HSPs must work more intentionally to avoid burnout, so it becomes necessary to have a toolkit of self-care practices.

PROTECTING YOUR ENERGY

One of the hallmarks of being human is the fact that our lives are often cyclical. When I started writing this book in December of 2022, I was amid seemingly endless Christmas parties. I had one for work, one for the different sides of my family, and several for friends. As the year progressed, the snow melted off, and daffodils bloomed. Wedding bells were in the air. (If you're in your 20s and 30s, you know that every year from May until August, there is a wedding nearly every weekend.)

Every year, without fail, I know I have to mentally

prepare myself for someone's nuptials. It's not that I don't like weddings; I am a dance floor *aficionado*. However, if it's a wedding for my second-cousin's sister-in-law, it often means I end up having to make small talk with strangers. These events can quickly become draining, and I've learned that I must learn how to protect my energy as an HSP at large functions.

If you find yourself constantly taking "bathroom breaks" at events, even though you don't really have to go, you probably know what I'm talking about. At large social gatherings, HSPs run the risk of their energy being drained by louder, more boisterous people. According to Dr. Judith Orloff, who's highly sensitive herself, HSPs must learn to defend and protect their sensitivity.

When HSPs fail to preserve their energy at social functions, they are left exhausted and in need of more intensive restoration. This can often cause HSPs to become hesitant to further socialize. This, too, becomes a vicious cycle and can lead to symptoms of depression and feelings of isolation. How, then, can HSPs prevent themselves from going from an engaged socialite to a jaded misanthrope?

HSPs can better maintain their energy by taking bathroom or "smoke" breaks at large gatherings. Even if you're not a smoker, taking a few minutes to step outside and take a few deep breaths will help you maintain your socializing endurance, thus preventing your energy from being depleted. While you take this smoke/bathroom break, spend some time practicing visualization. You could visualize a force field around you, protecting your energy from being stolen by non-sensitive people. You could also focus on "breathing in" peace and serenity while "breathing out" animosity and anxiety.

Lastly, before you arrive at the event, identify your socialization boundaries. If you can only be at a wedding for the reception and party entrance, that is fine! (Just make sure you say goodbye to the couple before you leave.) If you're going to a work Christmas party, set a time limit for the time you're willing to spend there. By implementing these boundaries (and sticking to them!), you'll notice you have the energy to go to gatherings, engage in your life, and make lasting memories while preserving your peace.

SLEEP HYGIENE

The irony of being an HSP is that we need more sleep than most, but many of us find it quite difficult to fall asleep. This is due to our over-analytical and anxious disposition. When our brains become overstimulated due to the emotional and environmental triggers we experience throughout the day, convincing our mind and body to settle down and rest becomes difficult. This acute or chronic daily stress can also lead to imbalanced cortisol levels.

Cortisol is a steroid hormone created by your endocrine glands which affect several bodily functions, particularly the body's stress responses. Cortisol also helps suppress inflammation, while too much can weaken your body's immune system. Your blood sugar and pressure are regulated by cortisol, as well. There are several life factors and diseases that can contribute to high cortisol. Symptoms of high cortisol include (but are not limited to) weight gain, muscle weakness, high blood sugar, and hypertension. If you think it wise to check your cortisol levels, I recommend consulting with your primary care physician.

Because HSPs are so sensory sensitive, they run a significant risk for cortisol and other hormone imbalance, thus leading to difficulty sleeping and an inability to recharge after social gatherings. Establishing a nightly routine is one way to help your brain and body destress and encourage sleep. This should be something easily repeatable, which you can do consistently. This routine will signal to your brain and body that it's time to wind down and prepare for a good night's sleep. Please note that this routine should include *limited screen time* as the blue light emitted from screens sends signals to your brain to be alert and active. Furthermore, you're risking the temptation to mindlessly scroll, which can severely limit your beauty sleep hours.

Try to identify hobbies you can do with your hands, such as Sudoku, reading, knitting, coloring, journaling, or sketching. You could also spend time cuddling your beloved pet. It's not really important *what* you do; it's just important to have a quiet, non-overstimulating activity.

Doing the same home or personal hygiene tasks each night will also help your brain unwind. For instance, I start my wind-down routine by doing the dishes each night. The repetition of this chore before bed tells my body it's time to begin getting ready for sleep. Maybe you're one of those people who has a 20-step skincare routine. This mindless routine will not only improve your skin but also tell your brain it's time to rest!

By establishing a nighttime routine, you'll notice that you have more energy to expend day-to-day. You'll be able to go to those larger social gatherings with a greater ability to protect your energy. Interacting with overly-chatty coworkers will become easier. Try implementing a nighttime routine for two-three weeks to see if you notice any improvement in your sleep habits.

EXERCISE AS TIME TO REFLECT AND RECHARGE

Often, when we think of meditating, we picture ourselves cross-legged and reciting "ohhhmm" for 90 minutes every day. While this may be perfect for some, it's just not going to work for most people. It is important to recognize that there are several ways you can practice mindfulness in your daily life, particularly by moving your body. Exercise, when done consistently, can promote both mental and physical health. And as mentioned previously, it will help condition you for life's stressors.

Humans tend to do better when they schedule 20-30 minutes a day to focus on movement. It helps modern-day people unplug from work and social media. Exercise can also help people manage acute and chronic stress and experience a more positive outlook on life. For HSPs, whose energy is more easily depleted, movement helps encourage and maintain physical and emotional energy. As you consistently exercise, you'll build muscle mass, thus increasing your endurance. This endurance will help spread oxygen to your body, thus increasing your lung and heart capacity, which leads to more energy.

Exercise promotes sleep, too. So, if you're looking to add a sleep routine to your life, it may be helpful to start exercising during the day. According to Johns Hopkins, exercise can help decrease insomnia by lowering your core body temperature and releasing endorphins. Their research suggests 30 minutes of aerobic activity per day can promote better sleep.

Additionally, regular exercise can promote a better outlook on life. It will help prevent conditions such as Heart Disease, Diabetes, and Depression.

As a highly sensitive young adult, you may struggle to get started with an exercise routine. This may be due to (understandable) lack of motivation, busy schedules, or gym anxiety. Fear not, my friend, for there are ways to get movement into your day without signing up for the Boston Marathon.

If you're in college or have a walkable commute, commit to leaving for class or work a little earlier to get some steps in. If you have a pet, take them on a morning and evening walk around the neighborhood. If you're in college, your university will likely have free exercise classes available to you; check them out to see if one interests you! It's important to remember to implement exercises to which you look forward to. If you hate running, don't try to become a runner. However, if you love riding your bicycle, commit to riding it a few days a week. Additionally, it may be helpful to schedule your exercise at the beginning of each week, which helps avoid decision fatigue and overwhelm.

It's important to remember that taking care of your physical and emotional health requires more than exercise. It also means that you schedule and attend regular doctor's appointments. It means drinking enough water and eating regularly. If the thought of completely overhauling your life seems overwhelming, fear not. Remember, a little goes a long way. A 10-minute walk is a great place to start. Drinking a glass of water in the morning, even better! You don't have to do it all at once; you have time to establish routines that will help support you in life. After all, we mustn't lose ourselves to self-betterment for self-betterment's sake. We are doing this to enjoy our lives, to participate in them. What's the point if you exercise for 3 hours every day but don't sleep at night? What's the point of sleeping 12 hours if you don't socialize? Work to find the balance that works for you and your lifestyle, and you'll notice increased energy and a better quality of life.

TAKING CARE OF YOUR MENTAL HEALTH

While exercising and sleeping are great practices to implement to support your mental health, there may be situations or feelings that can't be alleviated by a jog or a nap.

Part of creating an optimal self-care routine is utilizing several tools to encourage mental health and well-being. When I was younger, I was a habitual rollerblader. I didn't start blading to become fitter or to lose weight; I began rollerblading because I was angry and anxious, and it was the only way I knew how to flush out those feelings. There was nothing wrong with me using my blades as a coping mechanism. Actually, as far as coping mechanisms go, it's a pretty healthy one. However, when I mentioned this to my therapist, she informed me that it's important to have several ways to cope with such feelings, as I never know when a hobby could be taken away from me. While I could have taken that as a foreboding warning, I recognized what she was saying. We all need a tool kit, a coping skill book of recipes, if you will. There were some days when I was too tired to rollerblade; how was I coping with my anxiety? I had to identify other things that helped me cope. I started journaling and writing music, two things that kept my mind busy and prevented rumination.

Perhaps, for you, simply signing up for therapy would be helpful. You'll learn to accept and be given tools to cope with your feelings. You'll have a completely objective and well-trained listening ear with whom to discuss your life. It's slowly fading, I think, but there used to be a large stigma regarding counseling. Especially in the West, we think we must pull ourselves up by our bootstraps and press on. I'm here to say that this isn't true, and you can feel how you feel without punishing yourself.

We don't have to wait for things to get bad before we sign up for therapy, either. You don't have to experience a life-altering event before attending therapy. You can choose to attend therapy as a preventative measure or to discuss something that happened in the past that prevents you from moving on. Whatever the reason, attending therapy is a beneficial self-care practice for everyone. Don't get me wrong, it can be difficult to rehash old hurts, but it's a safe place to do so.

There may come a time when your mental and physical well-being could be supported by pharmacological therapy, as well. While it's not appropriate for everyone, your doctor or psychiatrist can help you determine the best treatment plan for you. If you've suffered from symptoms of depression and anxiety, or if you think you may be suffering from a different mental illness, I encourage you to discuss this with your therapist and doctor. As comedian Pete Davidson said,

> "There's no shame in the medicine game."

It may be difficult to know when it's important to seek help. However, if you're experiencing chronic insomnia, significant appetite changes, lack of interest in hobbies, inability to get out of bed in the morning, difficulty concentrating, or anything negatively impacting your life, please contact your doctor.

WHERE DO WE GO FROM HERE?

The world of self-care can be an overwhelming one. As of the publication of this book, if you Google self-care, you'll be met with 4.5 billion results. Needless to say, it's easy to get lost in the weeds when trying to figure out an individualized self-care routine. For HSPs, it's important to prioritize alone time to recharge, practice sleep hygiene, and prioritize physical and emotional health.

However, as mentioned before, self-care is about us, but it's also about our community. If we fail to rest and recharge, we offer the world the most exhausted and burnt-out version of ourselves. We may even begin to isolate ourselves due to our exhaustion. This, my friend, is not what life (or self-care) is about. When taking care of yourself, every practice you implement should answer the questions: Does this improve my quality of life? Does this practice allow me to show up as the best version of myself? If neither answer is yes, is it really "self-care," or is it something social media has been selling you as productive.

I've noticed an increase in the word "productive" on self-care social media posts, such as "My *Productive*

Morning Routine." So much so that I'm starting to think "productive" is just "hustle" masquerading as a healthy lifestyle choice. Well, I'm here to say self-care doesn't necessarily have to be productive. Self-care, really, is an act of defiance. It isn't choosing not to be productive; it is choosing to slow down and enjoy living your life. It's exercising, putting yourself to bed on time, spending time with loved ones, seeing new places, and savoring your favorite foods. Self-care is what happens when you make time to uninhibitedly be *you*.

HSPs spend a lot of their time focused on other people. We absorb others' feelings, emotions, and problems. We are the ever-present listeners, cheerleaders, and caregivers. Don't let the pursuit of caring for yourself become an obsession. Don't overthink it. Work to find a pocket of your day solely about doing something for the sheer joy of it. Play that video game, call your grandma while you're on a walk, badly decorate cupcakes. It's not about making or accomplishing something; it's about learning to enjoy the act of doing. To care for yourself is proclaiming, *"I'm worth it, too."*

JOURNAL PROMPTS

- *Reflect on a time when you felt overwhelmed and burned out. How did you try to cope with it? Did you prioritize self-care during that time? If not, what barriers prevented you from doing so?*

- *Consider your current approach to self-care. Do you tend to prioritize productivity over taking care of yourself? Reflect on the reasons behind your choices and how they affect your overall well-being. Are there any changes you would like to make in your self-care routine?*

- *How do you protect your energy as an HSP in social situations? Are there any specific strategies you use to maintain your socializing endurance and prevent your energy from being depleted? If not, what steps can you take to establish boundaries and protect your sensitivity?*

- *Explore your sleep habits and the challenges you face in getting restful sleep. Are there any nightly routines or activities that help you wind down and prepare for sleep? If not, what steps can you take to establish a calming routine that promotes better sleep hygiene for your sensitive nature?*

CONCLUSION

"Don't forget about the underrated songs, like Blue Jay Way," my dad solemnly advises, as he pops the Beatles' *Magical Mystery Tour* into his looming boom box and presses play. I quickly fiddle with my square blue mp3 player, pressing record. We had just figured out that the mp3 player I'd been given for my twelfth birthday had a record-setting, which led us to listen to the Beatles' discography. Outside, the sun quickly fades, giving way to a gray February winter sky. Snow is peacefully falling, and we're queuing up music to be recorded like a couple of radio DJs.

 My dad passed away not too long after, and I often mentally return to this quiet evening with him when I feel overwhelmed or anxious. Though simple, it is one of my favorite peaceful memories. It conjures up feelings utterly opposite to those I felt at Cedar Point. Instead of being surrounded by people, overwhelmed by extreme temperatures, and inundated with high-decibel noises, I felt relaxed and emotionally nourished.

If you're an HSP, the evening I've just described probably sounds ideal. With a penchant for peaceful, grounding hobbies, and quiet, more uncomplicated gatherings, you may often find yourself avoiding certain aspects of life. You may *want* to go to Cedar Point, a concert, or a football game, but the thought of having your delicate senses so shockingly assaulted keeps you from attending. I know what this feels like; trust me, I've been there.

The good news is there are ways to enjoy life as an HSP. With a little trial and error, practice, and dedication, you, too, can begin enjoying life as a person with sensory sensitivity. It may seem like you've been dealt a bad card by being born a highly sensitive person. However, I encourage you to view your sensitivity as a gift. As someone with a unique view of their surroundings, those close to you are lucky to have you. You have the ability to quickly stop and take in life as it is being lived. I have noticed that non-sensitive people often need a reminder to do so.

If, thus far, you feel as if your sensitivity has been

underappreciated, overlooked, or even criticized, know that there are people out there who will love you for who you are. Look for the people who give as much as they take, for it's easy to be steamrolled or taken advantage of as an HSP. This advice works well for employers and coworkers, as well.

Don't be afraid to be who you are, including at work. You don't have to hustle the most or be the top earner to contribute successfully to a team. You also don't have to work an endless amount of double shifts if you aren't able. By learning to identify your needs as an HSP, you'll become a better advocate for yourself. You'll know how to politely decline an extra project if you can't handle it. By learning to say no, you'll also be able to learn to say yes.

Often, overwhelmed HSPs lock themselves away in isolation when overwhelmed or burnt out. By learning to say no to things you don't physically or emotionally have the capacity for, you'll be able to say yes to the things that really matter to you but may require a bit more energy.

Additionally, when you inevitably do become burnt out, learn to care for yourself healthily. It can be tempting to binge-watch movies and endlessly scroll through media. This is fine; sometimes, this is even good. However, too much can exacerbate your feelings of overwhelm. It is important to establish coping mechanisms and self-care practices that feed your soul, nourish your body, and refresh your mind. Without these practices, you are more susceptible to the dreaded HSP sensory deluge.

One of the albums my dad and I recorded that February day was the Beatles' 1965 album *Rubber Soul*. Their song, *In My Life*, particularly spoke to me. In it, Lennon and McCartney write:

> *There are places I'll remember,*
> *all my life though some have changed,*
> *some forever, not for better,*
> *some have gone, and some remain*
>
> *All these places have had their moments,*
> *With lovers and friends, I still can recall,*
> *Some are dead, and some are living*
> *In my life, I've loved them all*

I have no conclusive evidence that any of the Beatles were or are highly sensitive, but in this song, they truly capture what it is to savor life. To acknowledge that sometimes it's hard, but when all is said and done, there is always the love we have for ourselves, our friends, and our family. Life is meant to be lived, not avoided. I hope this book has been the genesis of your journey to self-acceptance and growth as a highly sensitive person. It is my wish that you learn to love, accept, and take pride in your sensory sensitivity. I hope you use the tools provided in this book to fulfill the things you set out to accomplish. Lastly, I hope you continue to savor life and all it offers.

If you found value in reading my book, I would greatly appreciate it if you could spare a moment to leave a review on Amazon. Your feedback not only helps me grow as an author but also assists others in discovering and benefiting from the book. Thank you for your support!

ACKNOWLEDGMENTS

A heartfelt thank you goes out to Savannah for her hard work and dedication, and for always cheering me on! Without her, this book would never have been completed to this high-quality standard. I am truly and forever grateful.

JOURNAL PROMPTS

CHAPTER 1: THE TRUTH ABOUT BEING A HIGHLY SENSITIVE YOUNG ADULT

- *Reflect on a time when you had a strong intuition about someone or a situation, similar to the author's experience with David. What subtle cues or messages did you pick up on? How did your highly sensitive personality contribute to your ability to sense something was off?*

- *Explore your relationship with sensory sensitivity. Think about the different senses (sound, smell, taste, touch, sight) and how they affect you daily. Describe a specific situation where you felt overwhelmed or overstimulated by external* stimuli. How did you cope with it? Are there any strategies or techniques you can implement to manage sensory sensitivity in the future?

- Consider the benefits and challenges of being a highly sensitive person in today's society. What are some advantages of having enhanced sensory intake? On the other hand, what difficulties have you faced due to sensory sensitivity? How have these experiences affected your closest relationships and well-being?

- How did you come to realize that you have a highly sensitive personality? Reflect on the emotions and thoughts that surfaced when you discovered this aspect of your identity. How has this knowledge impacted your perception of yourself and your place in the world?

CHAPTER 2: I'M JUST A KID, AND LIFE IS (SOMETIMES) A NIGHTMARE

- *Reflect on a vivid childhood memory that is tied to a specific smell, texture, or sensory experience. Describe the memory and how it made you feel. How does this memory reflect your unique experiences as a child?*

- *Think about a time when you felt different or misunderstood compared to other children. How did this realization impact your self-perception and interactions with others? How did you navigate the challenges of being labeled as "different" or "sensitive"?*

- *Consider the unique traits of highly sensitive children provided by psychotherapist Jenna Fleming. Which of these traits resonate with you? How have these traits influenced your experiences? Reflect on how these traits can be seen as strengths rather than weaknesses.*

- *Reflect on a time when you faced a challenging situation that triggered your sensitivity. How did you react, and what emotions did you experience?*

How did you cope with the situation and process your feelings? Describe any strategies or coping mechanisms that helped you navigate your sensitivity.

CHAPTER 3: FOSTERING FULFILLING FRIENDSHIPS

- *Reflect on a time when your friends avoided communicating their thoughts or desires with you. How did this experience make you feel? How did you handle the situation?*

- *Have you ever been in a situation where you felt you gave more than you received from your close friends? Describe the dynamics of that friendship. How did it impact your well-being? What steps can you take to create a balanced and healthy friendship?*

- *Think about a friendship that you consider authentic and meaningful. What qualities does this friendship possess? How do you feel? What actions do you and your friend take to nurture this friendship?*

- *Reflect on emotional intelligence (EQ) and its importance in forming healthy friendships. How does your EQ influence your behavior and relationships? How do you recognize and understand emotions in yourself and others? Write down an example of a situation where your emotional intelligence played a significant role in a friendship.*

CHAPTER 4: ENRICHING ROMANTIC RELATIONSHIPS

- *Reflect on your past or current relationships and identify any patterns of communication that align with the strengths of highly sensitive people (HSPs) discussed in the chapter. How have these patterns affected your relationships positively or negatively?*

- *Explore the concept of identity fusion in romantic relationships. Have you ever experienced a merging of identities with your partner? How did it impact your relationship? Reflect on the potential challenges and benefits of identity fusion for HSPs.*

- *Consider the concept of emotional intimacy in relationships. How do you define emotional intimacy, and how important is it to you? Reflect on your capacity for emotional intimacy and how it aligns with being highly sensitive.*

- *Reflect on your past or current relationship and consider the strengths and challenges that arise from being a highly sensitive person (HSP). Think about how your verbal and nonverbal communication, empathy, conflict avoidance, and desire for emotional intimacy have influenced your relationship dynamics. Are there any patterns or behaviors that you have noticed? How do these strengths and challenges impact your overall relationship satisfaction?*

CHAPTER 5: CLAIMING CONTROL OF YOUR COLLEGE LIFE & LIVING SITUATIONS

- *Reflect on your past experiences living with others or in shared living situations. How have these experiences shaped your preferences and needs regarding cohabitation? Consider any challenges you faced and what you learned from them.*

- *Imagine yourself in a new living situation, such as a college dorm or a shared apartment. Create a list of your living preferences, including factors like noise levels, cleanliness, personal space, and social boundaries. How would these preferences contribute to your overall well-being and comfort?*

- *Think about your current living space or a space you feel comfortable in. Describe the elements that make it calming and comforting to you. How can you recreate or incorporate these elements in your future living situation to create a haven for yourself?*

- *Consider the concept of personal boundaries and how they apply to your college life. Identify one aspect of your life (such as study time, extracurricular involvement, or socializing) where you can set a clear boundary for yourself.*

Describe how this boundary will benefit your well-being and help you navigate the challenges of college life as a highly sensitive young adult.

∼

CHAPTER 6: PROSPER IN YOUR PROFESSIONAL LIFE

- *Reflect on your past experiences and the career paths you have considered. Have you ever felt pressured to choose a specific career based on societal expectations or the influence of others? How did that make you feel, and how did it impact your decision-making process?*

- *Consider the work environments that make you feel most comfortable and productive. Are any specific factors, such as noise levels, pace, or physical demands, significantly affecting your well-being in a work setting? How can you prioritize these factors when exploring potential career options?*

- *Explore your own definition of success in the workplace. How do you measure your success, and how does society influence these perceptions? How can you shift your focus from solely accomplishing tasks to prioritizing your well-being and how you feel while completing your work?*

- *Think about your experiences with performance reviews or evaluations. How do you typically react to feedback or critiques of your work? Are there any strategies you can employ to better navigate these situations as an HSP, keeping in mind that reviews of your work do not reflect your worth as an individual?*

CHAPTER 7: SQUASH SOCIAL MEDIA OVERWHELM

- *Reflect on your social media usage and its impact on your mental health. How often do you compare your life to others on social media? How does this comparison affect your self-esteem and overall well-being?*

- *Consider the strategies mentioned in the chapter for avoiding news overload. How do you currently consume news and feel overwhelmed by the constant barrage of information? How might implementing the suggestions in the chapter, such as limiting news intake and saying goodbye to negative influences, help improve your mental state?*

- *Explore your relationship with social media and the boundaries you have established. Are you in control of your social media use, or does it control you? How might you practice taking everything on social media with a grain of salt and focusing on accounts that make you feel represented or positive about yourself?*

- *Contemplate the concept of mindfulness and its potential benefits for your well-being. How often do you live in the present moment and appreciate the little things in life? Have you tried any mindfulness practices, such as meditation or movement, and how have they affected your overall mindset and stress levels?*

CHAPTER 8: EXPERIENCING THE MIND-BODY CONNECTION

- *Reflect on a time when you experienced a strong mind-body connection. Describe the emotions you were feeling and the physical symptoms that accompanied them. How did this experience affect your overall well-being?*

- *Consider your own thought patterns and cognitive distortions. Are there any recurring negative thoughts or beliefs you tend to fall into? Write them down and explore how they might be impacting your mental and physical health.*

- *Have you ever practiced writing down your negative thoughts and reframing them? If not, give it a try. Set aside a specific time of day to list your negative thoughts and then provide healthier alternatives or perspectives. How does this exercise make you feel?*

- *Explore the potential impact of your diet on your mental and physical health. Are there any specific foods or food groups you suspect might negatively affect you? Consider discussing this with a* healthcare provider and researching dietary approaches, such as the low FODMAP diet mentioned in the chapter. Reflect on any changes you could make to improve your well-being.

CHAPTER 9: EMBRACING SELF-CARE

- *Reflect on a time when you felt overwhelmed and burned out. How did you try to cope with it? Did you prioritize self-care during that time? If not, what barriers prevented you from doing so?*

- *Consider your current approach to self-care. Do you tend to prioritize productivity over taking care of yourself? Reflect on the reasons behind your choices and how they affect your overall well-being. Are there any changes you would like to make in your self-care routine?*

- *How do you protect your energy as an HSP in social situations? Are there any specific strategies you use to maintain your socializing endurance and prevent your energy from being depleted? If not, what steps can you take to establish boundaries and protect your sensitivity?*

- *Explore your sleep habits and the challenges you face in getting restful sleep. Are there any nightly routines or activities that help you wind down and prepare for sleep? If not, what steps can you take to establish a calming routine that promotes better sleep hygiene for your sensitive nature?*

ABOUT THE AUTHOR

Jordan T. Beckett is a dedicated author who has made it his mission to empower and uplift all through his inspiring books. As an avid researcher in psychology and personal development, Jordan is deeply committed to helping his readers navigate the challenges of adulthood with confidence.

Having experienced his fair share of ups and downs, Jordan brings a relatable and empathetic approach to his writing. He understands the struggles and pressures that people face in today's fast-paced world and is determined to provide them with the tools and strategies they need to overcome obstacles and thrive.

Through his books, Jordan combines practical advice, insightful anecdotes, and actionable steps to guide readers toward personal growth and success. He covers many topics, including self-esteem, goal setting, relationships, and mental well-being, offering invaluable wisdom that resonates with his audience.

Jordan's writing style is engaging and accessible,

making his books a joy to read for both seasoned self-help enthusiasts and those new to the genre. His genuine passion for peoples' well-being shines through every page, motivating and inspiring readers to take control of their lives and make positive changes.

When he's not writing, Jordan enjoys making music, spending time in nature, and connecting with his readers online. He believes in the power of human connection and strives to create a supportive community where everyone can thrive and find solace in their shared experiences.

Jordan T. Beckett empowers people to become their best versions through his heartfelt approach. His books are essential for anyone seeking guidance, motivation, and a roadmap to success in life's exciting and sometimes challenging journey.

Scan to explore more of his works!

BIBLIOGRAPHY

"The Highly Sensitive Person," n.d. https://hsperson.com/.

"Keeping Emotional Boundaries as a Highly Sensitive Person | HealthyPlace," April 26, 2021. https://www.healthyplace.com/blogs/relationshipsandmentalillness/2021/4/keeping-emotional-boundaries-as-a-highly-sensitive-person.

Agnew, Emily. "How to Get Yourself out of HSP Decision Paralysis - Sustainably Sensitive." Sustainably Sensitive, October 31, 2019. https://sustainablysensitive.com/how-to-get-yourself-out-of-hsp-decision-paralysis/.

Elaine. "Why Can't I Just Be Normal?," May 14, 2020. https://hsperson.com/why-cant-i-just-be-normal/.

Scott, Elizabeth, PhD. "What Is a Highly Sensitive Person (HSP)?" Verywell Mind, November 7, 2022. https://www.verywellmind.com/highly-sensitive-persons-traits-that-create-more-stress-4126393#:~:text=You.

Aron, Elaine N. "Introversion, Extroversion and the Highly Sensitive Person." Psychology Today, May 13, 2018. https://www.psychologytoday.com/us/blog/the-highly-sensitive-person/201805/introversion-extroversion-and-the-highly-sensitive-person.

Sólo, Andre, and Andre Sólo. "The Difference Between the Highly Sensitive Brain and the 'Typical' Brain - Sensitive Refuge." Sensitive Refuge - Your Sensitivity Is Your Greatest Strength. (blog), February 27, 2023. https://highlysensitiverefuge.com/highly-sensitive-person-brain/.

Georgetown Child & Family Counseling. "Highly Sensitive Child Traits – Child and Family Counseling Georgetown TX." Child & Family Counseling, October 11, 2022. http://www.jennaflemingcounseling.com/blog-post/traits-of-a-highly-sensitive-child/.

Junecao. "Highly Sensitive Child Requires Parenting Skills to Build

Resillience." Junhong (June) Cao, Ph.D., March 6, 2023. https://drjunhongcao.com/how-to-parent-your-highly-sensitive-child/.

Lmft, Brooke Nielsen, and Brooke Nielsen Lmft. "How Unhealed Trauma Affects Highly Sensitive People - Sensitive Refuge." Sensitive Refuge - Your Sensitivity Is Your Greatest Strength. (blog), December 23, 2021. https://highlysensitiverefuge.com/how-unhealed-trauma-affects-highly-sensitive-people/.

NCBI. "Understanding the Impact of Trauma," n.d. https://www.ncbi.nlm.nih.gov/books/NBK207191/#:~:text=Initial%20reactions%20to%20trauma%20can,effective%2C%20and%20self%2Dlimited.

"Trauma." Https://Www.Apa.Org, n.d. https://www.apa.org/topics/trauma.

CAMH. "20133 Trauma," n.d. https://www.camh.ca/en/health-info/mental-illness-and-addiction-index/trauma.

Lmft, Sara Ouimette. "The Highly Sensitive Person and Complex Trauma — Sara Ouimette, California Psychotherapy - Oakland, CA." Sara Ouimette, California Psychotherapy, January 21, 2023. https://www.saraouimette.com/blog/2018/6/10/the-hsp-and-c-ptsd-the-highly-sensitive-person-and-complex-trauma.

Website, Nhs. "Complex PTSD - Post-Traumatic Stress Disorder." nhs.uk, n.d. https://www.nhs.uk/mental-health/conditions/post-traumatic-stress-disorder-ptsd/complex/.

Leonard, Jayne. "What Is Complex PTSD: Symptoms, Treatment, and Resources to Help You Cope," December 23, 2022. https://www.medicalnewstoday.com/articles/322886#triggers.

Kennedy, Madeline, and Madeline Kennedy. "The Difference between CPTSD and PTSD and How to Treat Each Condition." Insider, May 26, 2022. https://www.insider.com/guides/health/mental-health/cptsd-vs-ptsd.

Center on the Developing Child at Harvard University. "Take the ACE Quiz – And Learn What It Does and Doesn't Mean - Center on the Developing Child at Harvard University," May 30, 2019. https://developingchild.harvard.edu/media-coverage/take-the-ace-quiz-and-learn-what-it-does-and-doesnt-mean/.

Starecheski, Laura. "Take The ACE Quiz — And Learn What It Does And Doesn't Mean." NPR, March 2, 2015. https://www.npr.org/sections/health-shots/2015/03/02/387007941/take-the-ace-quiz-and-learn-what-it-does-and-doesnt-mean.

Daines, Chantel, Dustin Hansen, M. Lelinneth B. Novilla, and AliceAnn Crandall. "Effects of Positive and Negative Childhood Experiences on Adult Family Health." BMC Public Health 21, no. 1 (April 5, 2021). https://doi.org/10.1186/s12889-021-10732-w.

PsyD, John M. Grohol. "How Your Past Can Help Guide Your Future." Psych Central, July 3, 2010. https://psychcentral.com/blog/how-your-past-can-help-guide-your-future#1.

Schwartz, Lance. "Bethany's Elevator Experiment a Case of Backward Research | Bethany Lutheran College." Bethany Lutheran College, December 6, 2022. https://blc.edu/2011/12/bethanys-elevator-experiment-a-case-of-backward-research/.

Pychology Today. "Conformity," n.d. https://www.psychologytoday.com/us/basics/conformity.

Bradberry, Travis. "9 Signs You're A Highly Sensitive Person." Forbes, August 30, 2016. https://www.forbes.com/sites/travisbradberry/2016/08/30/9-signs-youre-a-highly-sensitive-person/?sh=3d56c83662e3.

Callarman, Shannon, and Shannon Callarman. "The Unique Emotional Intelligence of Highly Sensitive People - Sensitive Refuge." Sensitive Refuge - Your Sensitivity Is Your Greatest Strength. (blog), September 9, 2022. https://highlysensitiverefuge.com/emotional-intelligence/.

Smith, Melinda, MA. "Improving Emotional Intelligence (EQ)." HelpGuide.Org, February 28, 2023. https://www.helpguide.org/articles/mental-health/emotional-intelligence-eq.htm.

Fraga, Juli. "Being a Highly Sensitive Person Is a Scientific Personality Trait. Here's What It Feels Like." Healthline, April 19, 2019. https://www.healthline.com/health/mental-health/what-its-like-highly-sensitive-person-hsp#2.-Being-an-HSP-affected-my-relationships.

Abs. "Tips for Making Friends as a Highly Sensitive Person and Build Healthy Relationships." A Beautiful Soul Holistic Counseling, June

26, 2021. https://beautifulsoulcounseling.com/tips-for-making-friends-as-a-highly-sensitive-person/.

Garza, Shannon. "Do Highly Sensitives Struggle More With Friendships?" HSP World, n.d. https://www.hsp.world/do-highly-sensitives-struggle-more-with-friendships/.

Barth, F. Diane. "How Do You Know If You Can Really Trust Someone?" Psychology Today, n.d. https://www.psychologytoday.com/us/blog/the-couch/202104/how-do-you-know-if-you-can-really-trust-someone.

"Home : Oxford English Dictionary," n.d. https://www.oed.com/.

"Tips for Making Friends as a Highly Sensitive Person and Build Healthy Relationships." A Beautiful Soul Holistic Counseling, June 26, 2021. https://beautifulsoulcounseling.com/tips-for-making-friends-as-a-highly-sensitive-person/.

Martin, Sharon. "Sharon Martin, DSW, LCSW Conquering Codependency GUILT 6 Ways to Set Boundaries Without Guilt." Psychology Today, n.d. https://www.psychologytoday.com/us/blog/conquering-codependency/202208/6-ways-set-boundaries-without-guilt#:~:text=Boundaries%20are%20limits%20and%20expectations,are%20no%20rules%20or%20guidelines.

mindbodygreen. "6 Types Of Boundaries You Deserve To Have (And How To Maintain Them)," December 13, 2022. https://www.mindbodygreen.com/articles/six-types-of-boundaries-and-what-healthy-boundaries-look-like-for-each.

Martin, Sharon. "Boundaries for the Highly Sensitive Person." Live Well With Sharon Martin, October 21, 2021. https://www.livewellwithsharonmartin.com/boundaries-highly-sensitive-person/.

Joho, Jess. "'Life Is Strange: True Colors' Review: An Evolution in Empathy Games." Mashable, October 29, 2021. https://mashable.com/article/life-is-strange-true-colors-review-empathy.

Tmcooper. "The Highly Sensitive Person and High Empathy." Dr. Tracy Cooper, April 8, 2015. https://drtracycooper.org/2015/04/08/the-highly-sensitive-person-and-high-empathy/.

Ward, Deborah. "The Highly Sensitive Person and the Narcissist." Psychology Today, n.d. https://www.psychologytoday.com/us/

blog/sense-and-sensitivity/201201/the-highly-sensitive-person-and-the-narcissist.

Rose, Cat, and Cat Rose. "4 Types of Unsafe Friendships for Highly Sensitive People - Sensitive Refuge." Sensitive Refuge - Your Sensitivity Is Your Greatest Strength. (blog), May 22, 2023. https://highlysensitiverefuge.com/unsafe-friendships/.

Martin, Sharon. "7 Types of Boundaries You Need to Set." The Better Boundaries Workbook, August 11, 2021. https://betterboundariesworkbook.com/types-of-boundaries/.

Phillips, Ashlee R. "Please Stop Using This Emily Brontë Quote as If It Is Romantic (It's Not)." Medium, May 6, 2018. https://medium.com/@smashlee011/please-stop-using-this-emily-bront%C3%AB-quote-as-if-it-is-romantic-its-not-ec14582298a7.

Sherman, Rose. "To Love a Highly Sensitive Person: A Theoretical Study on Romantic Relationships and Sensitivity." PDXScholar, n.d. https://pdxscholar.library.pdx.edu/honorstheses/394/.

Granneman, Jenn. "6 Strengths Highly Sensitive People Bring to Relationships." IntrovertDear.Com, July 12, 2018. https://introvertdear.com/news/strengths-highly-sensitive-people-bring-to-relationships/.

Ward, Deborah. 2019. "The HSP Relationship Dilemma." Psychology Today, August 15, 2019. https://www.psychologytoday.com/us/blog/sense-and-sensitivity/201802/the-hsp-relationship-dilemma.

Bjelland, Julie. "A Communication Tool Every HSP Needs to Learn — Julie Bjelland." Julie Bjelland, May 7, 2020. https://www.juliebjelland.com/hsp-blog/tools-to-help-sensitive-people-improve-relationships.

Healthline. "8 Things You Should Know About Dating a Highly Sensitive Person," April 7, 2021. https://www.healthline.com/health/relationships/dating-a-highly-sensitive-person-hsp#communication.

Me An INFP. "Difficulties of Being A Highly Sensitive Person [HSP] in College," June 25, 2020. https://www.youtube.com/watch?v=8ZsIRJ6jd0o.

Eby, Douglas. "27 Tips For Navigating College As a Highly Sensitive

Person." High Sensory Person, May 2, 2023. https://highlysensitive.org/284/27-tips-for-navigating-college-as-a-highly-sensitive-person/.

Liu, Peggy, and Peggy Liu. "7 Things I Wish My Family Knew About Me as a Highly Sensitive Person - Sensitive Refuge." Sensitive Refuge - Your Sensitivity Is Your Greatest Strength. (blog), April 26, 2019. https://highlysensitiverefuge.com/highly-sensitive-person-things-family-knew-about-me/.

Rivera, Sofia. "10 Tips for Finding a Roommate Who Doesn't Drive You Crazy." PODS Moving and Storage Blog, May 22, 2023. https://www.pods.com/blog/2020/06/finding-a-roommate/.

Trittin, Lauren, and Lauren Trittin. "How to Survive College as a Highly Sensitive Person - Sensitive Refuge." Sensitive Refuge - Your Sensitivity Is Your Greatest Strength. (blog), July 4, 2019. https://highlysensitiverefuge.com/how-to-survive-college-as-a-highly-sensitive-person/.

McFarlane, David Michael. "10 Easy Ways To Create Personal Space In Your Apartment." Elbow Room, December 2, 2019. https://www.clutter.com/blog/posts/create-personal-space/.

"How to Survive College as a Highly Sensitive Person - Sensitive Refuge." Sensitive Refuge - Your Sensitivity Is Your Greatest Strength. (blog), July 4, 2019. https://highlysensitiverefuge.com/how-to-survive-college-as-a-highly-sensitive-person/.

Eby, Douglas. 2023. "27 Tips For Navigating College As a Highly Sensitive Person." High Sensory Person, May. https://highlysensitive.org/284/27-tips-for-navigating-college-as-a-highly-sensitive-person/.

Ishler, Julianne. "Sleep Tips for the Highly Sensitive Person." Healthline, August 12, 2021. https://www.healthline.com/health/sleep/sleep-tips-for-the-highly-sensitive-person#sleep-obstacles.

Minkoff, Peter. "Difficulties Students Can Face Being a Highly Sensitive Person in College - High Style Life." High Style Life, April 13, 2021. https://highstylife.com/difficulties-students-can-face-being-a-highly-sensitive-person-in-college/.

Sólo, Andre, and Andre Sólo. "The 7 Best Careers for a Highly Sensitive Person - Sensitive Refuge." Sensitive Refuge - Your Sensitivity Is Your Greatest Strength. (blog), May 4, 2023. https://highlysensitiverefuge.com/highly-sensitive-person-careers/.

Sólo, Andre, and Andre Sólo. "7 Workplace Problems Only Highly Sensitive People Will Understand - Sensitive Refuge." Sensitive Refuge - Your Sensitivity Is Your Greatest Strength. (blog), March 7, 2020. https://highlysensitiverefuge.com/work-problems-highly-sensitive-people/.

Kelly. "9 Tips for Coping in the Workplace as a Highly Sensitive Person | A Highly Sensitive Person's Life," n.d. https://highlysensitiveperson.net/tips-coping-workplace-job-career-highly-sensitive-person/.

Bass, Bianca. "How Being a Highly Sensitive Person Can Make You More Successful." Medium, December 13, 2021. https://medium.com/the-post-grad-survival-guide/how-being-a-highly-sensitive-person-can-make-you-more-successful-758ede87884.

Lee, Clarisse, and Clarisse Lee. "How to Actually Get Stuff Done as a Highly Sensitive Person - Sensitive Refuge." Sensitive Refuge - Your Sensitivity Is Your Greatest Strength. (blog), January 19, 2019. https://highlysensitiverefuge.com/procrastination-highly-sensitive-person/.

Lpcc, Rupali Grover, and Rupali Grover Lpcc. "Why Highly Sensitive People Sometimes React So Strongly to Criticism - Sensitive Refuge." Sensitive Refuge - Your Sensitivity Is Your Greatest Strength. (blog), December 17, 2019. https://highlysensitiverefuge.com/highly-sensitive-people-criticism/.

"Why It's Important to Take Career Risks in Your 20s," n.d. https://www.upskilled.edu.au/skillstalk/important-to-take-career-risks-in-your-20s.

Harwin, Cliff. "Highly Sensitive People/Introverts: How Does Your Comfort Zone Help You?," n.d. https://www.thehighlysensitiveperson.com/highly-sensitive-people-introverts-how-does-your-comfort-zone-help-you/.

Work - Chron.com. "Tips for Highly Sensitive People to Find a Job,"

November 21, 2017. https://work.chron.com/tips-highly-sensitive-people-job-17494.html.

"Differences In The HSP Brain, By Julie Bjelland, LMFT — Julie Bjelland." Julie Bjelland, March 10, 2021. https://www.juliebjelland.com/hsp-blog/2017/3/23/differences-in-the-hsp-brain-by-julie-bjelland-lmft.

Mayo Clinic. "Meditation: A Simple, Fast Way to Reduce Stress," April 29, 2022. https://www.mayoclinic.org/tests-procedures/meditation/in-depth/meditation/art-20045858#:~:text=Meditation%20can%20produce%20a%20deep,physical%20and%20emotional%20well%2Dbeing.

Ncc, Carolyn Cole Lcpc, Lmft, and Carolyn Cole Lcpc Ncc Lmft,. "5 Cognitive Distortions HSPs May Experience - Sensitive Refuge." Sensitive Refuge - Your Sensitivity Is Your Greatest Strength. (blog), August 17, 2021. https://highlysensitiverefuge.com/5-cognitive-distortions-hsps-may-experience/.

Stewart, Lauren. "How HSPs Can Deal With Negative Emotions (And Actually Feel Better)." IntrovertDear.Com, February 26, 2021. https://introvertdear.com/news/negative-emotions-highly-sensitive-person/.

Vee, Vicky, and Vicky Vee. "My HSP Struggle With Depression — and the Road to Healing - Sensitive Refuge." Sensitive Refuge - Your Sensitivity Is Your Greatest Strength. (blog), January 9, 2021. https://highlysensitiverefuge.com/depression/.

Orloff, Judith, MD. 2020. "The Effect of Medication on Sensitive People." Psychology Today, January 10, 2020. https://www.psychologytoday.com/us/blog/the-empaths-survival-guide/201805/the-effect-medication-sensitive-people.

"AboutKidsHealth," n.d. https://www.aboutkidshealth.ca/article?contentid=3667&language=english.

Pestano, Aimee Barnes. "The Highly Sensitive Body: Handle With Care — Tangram Wellness." Tangram Wellness, July 12, 2017. https://tangramwellness.com/blog//the-highly-sensitive-body-handle-with-care.

Bates, Jordan. "'Letting Go' by David Hawkins: The Book That Shifted

My Entire Reality." Jordan Bates, May 13, 2020. https://jordanbates. life/letting-go-david-hawkins/.

The Healing Room Donabate. "Vitamin B6, Emotional Sensitivity and Nutrition - The Healing Room, Donabate." The Healing Room, Donabate - Reiki Healing, Angel Card Readings and Counselling. (blog), August 1, 2022. https://healingroomdublin.net/wp/vitamin-b6-emotional-sensitivity-and-nutrition/.

Anastasia. "The Impact of Food Intolerances on Mental Health." Food for the Brain, January 26, 2022. https://foodforthebrain.org/the-impact-of-food-intolerances-on-mental-health/.

Orloff, Judith, MD, and Judith Orloff MD. "6 Tips for Highly Sensitive People and Empaths to Protect Their Energy - Sensitive Refuge." Sensitive Refuge - Your Sensitivity Is Your Greatest Strength. (blog), February 2, 2019. https://highlysensitiverefuge.com/highly-sensitive-people-empaths-protect-energy/.

Scheib, Emma, and Emma Scheib. "Why Highly Sensitive People May Need More Sleep Than Others - Sensitive Refuge." Sensitive Refuge - Your Sensitivity Is Your Greatest Strength. (blog), January 15, 2020. https://highlysensitiverefuge.com/highly-sensitive-people-sleep/.

Sugar, Jenny. "What Is the Best Workout For a Highly Sensitive Person? | What Is a Highly Sensitive Person, Or..." POPSUGAR Fitness, June 11, 2021. https://www.popsugar.com/fitness/photo-gallery/48030888/image/48068788/What-Is-Best-Workout-For-Highly-Sensitive-Person?fullsite=1.

Prober, Paula, and Paula Prober. "16 Ways to Calm the Heck Down When You're a Highly Sensitive Overthinker - Sensitive Refuge." Sensitive Refuge - Your Sensitivity Is Your Greatest Strength. (blog), November 28, 2020. https://highlysensitiverefuge.com/how-to-calm-down-overthinker/.

Rice, Shaun, and Shaun Rice. "5 Grounding Techniques for Overstimulated HSPs - Sensitive Refuge." Sensitive Refuge - Your Sensitivity Is Your Greatest Strength. (blog), May 9, 2020. https://highlysensitiverefuge.com/5-grounding-techniques/.

goop. 2017. "Why Navigating Your 20s Is Hard." Goop, August. https://goop.com/wellness/career-money/navigating-20s-hard/.

Cole, Nicolas. "9 Things You Should Start Doing In Your 20s To Guarantee You'Ll Be Successful." Minutes - Insights From the Internet's Brightest Minds., July 10, 2019. https://minutes.co/9-things-you-should-start-doing-in-your-20s-to-guarantee-youll-be-successful/.

Valko, Lauren, and Lauren Valko. "18 Things That Fill Highly Sensitive People With Joy - Sensitive Refuge." Sensitive Refuge - Your Sensitivity Is Your Greatest Strength. (blog), May 4, 2023. https://highlysensitiverefuge.com/things-that-fill-highly-sensitive-people-with-joy/.

"HSPs Need Creative Outlets! | A Highly Sensitive Person's Life," n.d. https://highlysensitiveperson.net/creative/.

Johns Hopkins Medicine. "Exercising for Better Sleep," August 8, 2021. https://www.hopkinsmedicine.org/health/wellness-and-prevention/exercising-for-better-sleep.

"The Highly Sensitive Person: How to Thrive When the World Overwhelms You," 1991.

Printed in Great Britain
by Amazon